The Shakespeare Conundrum

An Independent Inquiry into the Truth about Shakespeare

Other books by E. C. Ayres

Tony Lowell Mysteries
Hour of the Manatee
Eye of the Gator
Night of the Panther
Lair of the Lizard
Day of the Red Tide

Jake Fleming Investigations
A Tigers Heart
When Darkness Falls
Black Dragon River

Young Adult
Toon Man

Non-Fiction
The Shakespeare Conundrum
Inside the New China

The Shakespeare Conundrum

An Independent Inquiry into
the Truth about Shakespeare

E.C. Ayres

SPEAKING VOLUMES, LLC
NAPLES, FLORIDA
2021

The Shakespeare Conundrum

Cover design by Hannah Linder

ISBN 978-1-64540-417-0

Prologue

Setting the Stage

In 1951, an obscure English author named Elizabeth MacKintosh, writing as Josephine Tey, published an extraordinary short novel (188 pages, once again proving that size isn't everything) which legendary New York Times book critic Anthony Boucher declared to be "one of the permanent classics in the detective field." Boucher further proclaimed Tey's modest little novel to be "not only one of the best mysteries of the year, but of all time." Such praise was not lightly given by the redoubtable Mr. Boucher, or for that matter, any book reviewer, just on general principles. Interestingly, Boucher's use of the phrase "of all time" echoes Ben Jonson's words three hundred and fifty years earlier to describe Shakespeare. In a eulogy written several years after the death of the Bard, Jonson called him ". . . a man for all time." Of course, Jonson was just parroting Robert Whittington's eulogy for the sainted Thomas More, "a man for all seasons." Which like everything else we think we know, may or may not have been true. Which, when it comes to Shakespeare, is the whole point of this book.

Tey's little novel was titled *The Daughter of Time*, the title originating not with Jonson, nor, for that matter Shakespeare, but from an old proverb: "Truth is the daughter of time." And what Tey had done was, if not alter history, at least alter the public's *perception* of history, and open up to legitimate question a matter that had long been thought laid to rest: the truth regarding the alleged villainy of King Richard III, and the murder of the two princes in the Tower of London. What Tey dared to suggest, through the literary device of present day detective work, was that Richard was not at all the hunchbacked demon depicted by Sir

Thomas More on behalf of the Tudor dynasty that succeeded him, and that he had very likely been slandered, not to mention murdered (at Bosworth Field) by the French-born adventurer Henry Tudor (Henry VII), a distant cousin of his mother.

Tey's book is a fascinating and entertaining page turner, in which a passive, bedridden police detective takes up the cause of the deposed king Richard, triggered at first purely by a casual perusal of a copy of his portrait, the original of which still hangs in the National Gallery. This portrait depicts—in the view of our querulous policeman accustomed, it seems, to making snap judgments—a thoughtful, sad, intelligent man, who has seen much travail, and had tried to do the right thing. We all know where that can get you, who live in the 21st Century (the same place it tended to get you in any other century).

Charmed into passive curiosity by that alluring visage, our fictional detective begins to send for documents: the "Sainted" Thomas More's history, Parliament's Act of Attainder giving Richard the rightful throne, Richard's own letters, Stillington's testimony, Henry VII's overturning of the Bill of Attainder and orders to burn all copies (which failed), and in so doing makes the uncomfortable discovery that there was no evidence the boys had in fact vanished at all, prior to the overthrow and death of Richard.

Piece by piece Tey's detective builds his case, at first inspired solely by the portrait, but subsequently construing, from historical documents, that Richard had been framed, not surprisingly by Henry VII: the beloved inventor of the Star Chamber and father of the equally venomous if more charming Henry VIII. Henry VII also invented the concept of judicial murder, by means of which he successfully eliminated, one by one, all other legitimate heirs to the crown of Edward III, and in fact, the entire York line of succession.

Alas, poor York. After which, of course, the coup was complete and irrevocable, new histories were written to laud Henry's actions, and became established, over time, as "fact." As Mark Twain so aptly put it, history is merely "lies, agreed upon." Indeed.

In carrying out his supine investigation, Josephine Tey's police detective found an interesting contemporary analogy to the case of King Richard, in a phenomenon known in British lore as "Tonypandy." This was a term based on an incident in the early 1900's, in which British government troops massacred a striking band of coal miners in South Wales. Except, they didn't. No one was actually killed that day, or even wounded (either the troops were terribly poor shots, or no shots were actually fired). Nonetheless, the incident became a rallying cry for all Welshmen good and true for decades thereafter, and fact became overwritten by legend, until a completely untrue story became common knowledge, "while the men who knew it to be untrue," as Tey's investigator complained, "looked on and said nothing."

History is chock-full of "Tonypandy" of that sort, of course: events that become distorted, twisted, or completely perverted by interested authorities (such as the Tudors, or say, Hollywood) and ensuing scholars in their behalf, for whatever reason (surely never power or money), until facts are ignored or discarded, evidence rejected or destroyed, and legend becomes the new paradigm.

All of which brings to mind the strange and compelling case of William Shakespeare, our beloved Bard. Scholars, academics, and subsequent powerful economic interests have, over the past three centuries and more, ingeniously and successfully raised an illiterate glover's son from Stratford-on-Avon to the stature of a literary deity, without any evidence of his actually having written anything at all, let alone the plays, other than the unfortunate fact that someone ascribed his name to them (presumably he, himself), much the way early Hollywood film producers imprinted their names on the movies. Despite protestations from as diverse a collection of disbelievers as Mark Twain and Samuel Taylor Coleridge (also, for the martially inclined, the not-easily buffaloed Otto Von Bismarck), this flimsy bit of circumstantial evidence was apparently sufficient in the eyes of England's historians and scholars to declare the matter settled "for all time" and slam the door on further inquiry. Much as Thomas More did to the memory of the last Richard Plantagenet.

Were it not for the fact that this was, well, Shakespeare, such an implausible scenario would have been rendered to the nearest dustbin, forthwith and for good, a long time ago. Yet those so willing to accept Shakespeare's claim willy-nilly and without question have been obliged to either ignore or suppress a large and growing body of evidence that piquantly suggests that pretty much anybody *except* Shakespeare could have written the Canon. As in Tey's case for Richard, a reasonably competent modern-day detective would quickly construe, from such evidence as exists, a troubling and intriguing pattern: one that strongly indicates that, in fact, the legend of Shakespeare's rise from humble origins is nothing but *Tonypandy*.

William Shakspeare (his real name was Shakspur, or one of a number of variations thereof) was already established as the Elizabethan equivalent of a small-time agent/producer (he would soon own ten percent of the theater company) when one of London's leading playwrights, Robert Greene, let loose with a blast of accusatory invective (from his deathbed) called *A Groatsworth of Wit*, calling Shakespeare a host of names, none of them complimentary. Greene was evidently miffed about not getting paid (ah, such malcontents, we writers!) and was trying to warn the rest of the theatrical world as early as 1592, to watch out for a certain "Jack of All Trades" named "Shakescene," whose dealings were apparently less than above-board.

Apparently no one listened. Greene accused "Shakescene" of being a clever, manipulative, and thoroughly unprincipled agent, broker, and plagiarist, among other things. Shakespearean scholars have happily embraced "Shakescene" as being their own, without feeling the need to address or acknowledge any of the unpleasant things that Greene actually said about him.

Shakespeare was clearly a shrewd and successful businessman: grounds enough, apparently, to embrace his claims of authorship, in the eyes of academe. He was, in established fact, a theatrical entrepreneur, who, in addition to money lending, costume brokering and real estate investment, acquired, performed in, owned, produced, and published plays. Many plays. In other words, a producer! He somehow acquired those thirty-six extraordinary works in the Canon, and many more besides, some of them appallingly bad (another embarrassment scholars tend to gloss over, or simply avoid discussing). But there is no evidence at all that he ever *wrote* any of them.

From the perspective of one familiar with the shenanigans of the denizens of Hollywood, and (at least in this sense like Tey) a writer with a modicum of understanding of basic investigative procedures, it seems entirely possible that somebody, over a long period of time, has very seriously dropped the ball, regarding Shakespeare.

The truth about Shakespeare, deplorable as it may sound, might actually be something as simple and plain as the ruddy well-fed face affixed to his Stratford bust: a story made for Hollywood. Picture if you will, the setting: rural byways and backwaters of Elizabethan England, where pigs and sheep outnumber books ten thousand to one, and education is all but unheard of. On the horizon we see the outline of a small farm town, like any other in this primitive, bucolic countryside. On closer scrutiny, we descry a glover's workshop dominating the village center, with stucco walls, a red tile roof, and diagonal beams across the front, an architectural precursor to the Union Jack, complete with aromatic sludge pond around back. Alongside, in similar rustic edifices stand a butcher's shop, a baker's shop, a tavern, and above all a spired stone church, with a rectory and a small school tucked in among the fields for religious instruction. A few farms lie beyond, with thatched roofs and barns, then rolling farmlands, then hills finally giving way to forest. King Henry VIII is dead and gone, but his Church of England now governs in all matters of religion. His spinster daughter Elizabeth reigns with a firm hand over the secular Kingdom. A plot is brewing, because a good story must have a plot: the Virgin Queen's half-sister Mary yearns for freedom and her own right to the crown, of both her own Catholic-dominated Scotland, but also Protestant England as well.

Some people just can't settle for half-way measures. War is imminent, and the Medicis are plotting to seize control over all of Europe, including the British Isles, and eliminate the Protestant scourge once and for all.

Of course, the people of the farming town of Stratford know little of this, and couldn't care less. They are busy growing crops, and slaughtering hogs, and selling their produce on the London road. One local youth, already a handful to the town constable, has a bit of a nasty habit—poaching deer on neighboring lands. He's a character of sorts, more inclined to skipping school than attending it, to roaming neighboring farms aspiring to greater things, entertaining the customers at the local butcher shop where he apprentices with bits of doggerel, flirting with the farm girls thereabouts.

His family is ignorant. They, like their neighbors, know nothing of the struggles in Europe or elsewhere, having never traveled so far as London, let alone overseas. Nor will the young lad venture further than London, ever in his lifetime. Scotland is unknown to him except perhaps in legend; Latin is an alien tongue spoken rarely and only for purposes of religious instruction; Greek is unknown, Ovid unheard of, and books non-existent. No matter. Clearly, as history tells us, the boy was a genius! And genius, like life itself, will find a way.

Young Will Shakspur, the glover's son, has a propensity for composing those bits of doggerel in his head, some say (or said long after), as well as petty thievery, and is skilled with puppets, and with negotiating a tough bargain. He is illiterate, but then, so are his parents, and brothers, as will remain his wife and all of his children. Far more importantly, he has a good head for business.

After impregnating a local girl whom he is obliged to marry, then quickly rendering her barefoot and pregnant twice more in a matter of three years, and with his reputation for poaching dogging him, and perhaps visions of grander schemes in mind, young Will Shakspur flees town, works for a time in Lancastershire as a puppeteer (or at least somebody named "Will Shake-scene" did), then finally sojourns south to London to make his fortune.

He starts modestly enough, drawn to the theater but lacking the necessary skills, other than for sweeping the galleries after each performance, emptying slop buckets and scrubbing the stage. But it's a start. Observing, after a time, that many theater patrons arrive on horseback with nowhere to stable their mounts, young Will recognizes opportunity, and seizes it by the reins, literally. He quickly corners the horse-grooming market at Burbage's Theater in Shoreditch, and soon has a stable of his own of young boys willing to work for a groat, holding horses for the dandies while the play goes on. "Shakespeare's Boys," they become known as: clearly the precursors to the present day phenomenon known as "valet parking!" Newly affluent, our enterprising Will seizes upon another opportunity that arises. The plague has fallen upon London, and many of the theaters are forced to close. Desperate for money, starving actors sell their costumes—for pennies—to the ambitious young rustic who has already established himself as a moneylender, and will soon own ten percent of the theater. That's when young Will takes an interest in the plays. Play scribblers abound in London, all those University Wits, desperate to ply their craft and/or feed themselves: Robert Greene, Thomas Nash, George Chapman, Thomas Kyd, Kit Marlowe and others. Already skilled at brokering costumes, and then loans, it is a natural progression for the rising theatrical entrepreneur to begin brokering plays. He is positioned in the front office. He considers himself a dabbler, as well as an actor. He is stationed there at the transom, over which all plays submitted to the Company must pass.

He begins to buy them, and to represent the authors to the Company, always for a percentage, of course. The Company, (then he himself) becomes "owner," and the plays are usually produced anonymously: a presentation of the Admiral's Men, or Lord Strange, or Pembroke's Players, or the other patrons of the time. Much like Hollywood, London theaters become an industry. The Company controls the plays, and the writers, whenever possible, are exploited, then discarded. Eventually, the ungrateful Greene complains about this state of affairs, and dies shortly thereafter in poverty, under questionable circumstances. Authors' rights, apparently, do not exist in Elizabethan London. As with Hollywood, especially in the early years, the producers own all, control all, claim or bestow the credits as they like, and keep all the profits. (As a sidebar, one should note that even today, screenwriters are excluded from copyright protection thanks to a deal hammered out between the producers and their friends in congress in those storied early years of Hollywood, in exchange for allowing writers to form a union. Of course, to keep things in balance, the same deal prohibits book authors from collective bargaining!).

Writers in the Elizabethan theater, like Hollywood, are merely workers for hire, whose craft is valued little more than that of the stage carpenter, or set designer, or costume broker in the hearts, eyes, and minds of the theater public. The *play* is the thing.

Then, in 1587, a new phenomenon appears on the literary horizon: a poetic comet who streaks across the smudged and darkened London sky and renders all else written up until then as insignificant, the flickering of guttering torches in the night. This new poet is the first playwright to become a true star of the London stage, leader of the Cambridge "University Wits," continental spy for Thomas Walsingham and Lord Burghley, and member of Sir Walter Raleigh's notorious round table of free thinkers, the "School of Night." And Will Shakspur, the up-and-coming working-class entrepreneur, envies him (despite their nearly identical social origins), and by 1593 sees exactly how to use him, for his own everlasting personal gain.

Now, all that's missing is murder! . . . .

PART ONE

THE MAN WHO INVENTED HOLLYWOOD

Chapter One

A war of Words

In his essay on the power of surmise, *Is Shakespeare Dead*? Mark Twain once described how Shakespearean scholars have had to work backwards from that single, diaphanous piece of evidence (a name on a title page) to make their case for William Shakespeare as author of the Canon that bears his name. Imagine the contortions those Stratfordian savants have had to undergo to bend the facts to fit their thesis!

Instead of sticking to the evidence, or resorting to logic, they insist that, because "Shakespeare" clearly understood law, for example, he "must have been" apprenticed to a lawyer at one time or another, in his life before London. Not that there is any evidence of this at all, which there is not. Their thinking goes roughly as follows:

Shakespeare's name was on the Folio and some of the Quartos. Ergo, he must have written them. The author clearly had a vast store of knowledge, connections, background, talent, and wisdom to have done so. Therefore Shakespeare must have had a fine education. And since he never went to any schools that we know of, he must have taught himself. And since he must have taught himself, he must have had books. And since his will included no trace of or reference to any books or other literary materials among the considerable personal property accumulated in his lifetime, he must have borrowed some.

But since books alone would not provide the vocabulary and detailed knowledge of Europe, Scotland, England and Kent that we find in the plays, he must have gone there. And since there is no evidence he went there, he must have talked to or corresponded with people who did go there. And since there is no record of him hobnobbing or other business matters, those particular records must have been lost.

All of which somehow proves, beyond a shadow of a doubt, that Shakespeare must have written the plays!

This is the reasoning of the orthodox Shakespeareans, who have stifled all dissent on this issue from the very beginning. One shudders to think what, say, Johnny Cochrane might have done with such reasoning, on the witness stand. As Mark Twain observed in his essay, what they did was surmise what "must be" true, which somehow became, in their view, fact. And having taken this position, they have bolstered it with a fortress of ideology that would rebuff an armada.

As Mark Twain put it:

"So far as anyone knows and can prove, Shakespeare of Stratford-on-Avon never wrote a play in his life.

"o far as anyone knows and can prove, he never wrote a letter to anybody in his life.

"So far as anyone knows, he received only one letter during his life [The Quiney letter from a Stratford neighbor requesting a loan].

So far as anyone knows and can prove, Shakespeare of Stratford wrote only one poem during his life. This one is authentic. He did write that one—a fact which stands undisputed; he wrote the whole of it; he wrote the whole of it out of his own head. He commanded that this work of art be engraved upon his tomb, and he was obeyed. There it abides to this day. This is it:

Good friend for Iesus sake forbeare,
To digg the dust encloased heare:
Blest be ye man yt spares thes stones
And curst be he yt moves my bones. *(sic)"*

This was it? The final statement from the man who wrote: *Othello* and *Macbeth*? How tragic. At least he could have added: *"To be or not to be!"*

Given this sort of nonsensical evidence, it's no surprise that for the last two centuries, there has been a deep and abiding suspicion that something was wrong with this picture. Consider the portrait of the all-wise Bard holding quill and paper, so firmly etched in the minds of all Western-educated students of literature, including yours truly. What no one would venture to suggest, above a whisper, was the faint yet growing suspicion that, should one dare to peek between one's fingers, *the emperor wore no clothes*! The famous bust of William Shakespeare smirking from his Stratford pedestal with his empty eyes, ruddy cheeks and re-done hand props itself speaks a myth. The original bust was that of an agrarian burgher, holding a sack of grain, which a latter-day True Believer altered to project the more suitable image of the poet, which he had somehow become. Here is what some of the greatest minds of all time have had to say on the subject of Shakespeare's veracity:

"The bard play-writing in his room, The bard a humble clerk, The bard, a lawyer, parson, groom, The bard, deer-stalking after dark, The bard a tradesman—and a Jew— The bard a botanist—a beak— The bard a skilled musician, too— A sheriff and a surgeon, eke!" William S. Gilbert

W.S. Gilbert (of Gilbert and Sullivan) was hardly alone among the giants of literature to express reservations, often bordering on the incredulous, as to the legitimacy of Shakespeare's claim:

Ask your own hearts, ask your own common sense, to conceive the possibility of the author of the plays being the anomalous, the wild, the

irregular genius of our daily criticism. What! Are we to have miracles in sport? Does God choose idiots by whom to convey divine truths to man? Samuel Taylor Coleridge

Any man who believes that William Shakespeare of Stratford wrote Hamlet or Lear is a fool. John Bright

It would be a positive relief to me to dig him up and throw stones at him. George Bernard Shaw

I am . . . haunted by the conviction that the divine William is the biggest and most successful fraud ever practiced on a patient world. Henry James

I cannot marry the facts of William Shakespeare's life to his supposed authorship of the greatest plays and poems in the history of the world." Ralph Waldo Emerson

Interestingly, it was Emerson who wrote:

Daughters of Time, the hypocritic days,
Muffled and dumb, like barefoot dervishes . . . .

The point is, these doubts are expressed by renowned scholars and authors with proven records of accomplishment in their own right. Unlike the man alleged to be the "Bard." Those notables sensed something amiss about Shakespeare a long time ago. Many subsequent writers and scholars, perhaps too polite to speak out in sufficiently forceful terms to get the public's attention, have been convinced for decades that the man from Stratford was a fraud. One wouldn't know it, living as we do in the shadow of the New Globe Theater in London, the Stratford tourist megalopolis, the Folger Shakespeare Library, countless Shakespeare Festivals, and the mighty edifices of academe presiding *uber alles*. But William Shakespeare's actual *proven* writing career is sharply, clearly and solely defined by that single bit of graveyard doggerel derided by Mark Twain. A reasonably competent detective such as Josephine Tey's Alan Grant would be forced to at least suspect, if not conclude, from this evidence alone, that the man who wrote that fatuous epitaph wrote little else.

Fortresses, unfortunately, tend to endure for a very long time. Not that they haven't had to withstand the occasional assault. The initial breach in the Stratfordians' (Shakespeareans') formidable palisade of public acceptance broke through with the first of Sir George Greenwood's startling books, *The Shakespeare Problem Revisited*, published in 1908. Greenwood followed with two more books before the academic drawbridge came thundering down, and the overwhelming forces of orthodoxy were sent charging out against him.

In brief, while in retreat he had this to say about Shakespeare:

My last comment on the life of William Shakespeare of Stratford shall be this. Meager as our knowledge of it is, it is yet too much. (Sir Sidney) Lee's claim that we have a 'mass of biographical detail which far exceeds that of any poet contemporary with Shakespeare' is indeed sufficiently ridiculous, but it would be far better for the Stratfordian theory if we had no biographical detail at all. If we knew nothing we might imagine anything. What we do know is fatal to the case. It gives rise to the strongest possible presumption against the identity of Shakespeare the player with Shakespeare the poet.

In other words, whatever documentation Shakespeare's preeminent proponent Sir Sidney Lee was citing, it didn't include any evidence at all that Shakespeare was a poet or playwright. Oddly, this remains as true today as it was a century ago. One can picture alarms going off in Sergeant Grant's head. They certainly went off in mine when I read this.

Nevertheless, the Stratfordians had won, mainly by the combined powers of tradition and attrition. Also because Greenwood had no one else to offer up in Shakespeare's place except Frances Bacon, who was a great religious scholar and learned man, but no poet. Nor did he ever claim to be a poet, and had no cause to conceal such a fact even if he had been. The vast majority of documentary evidence existent in Shakespeare's biography mostly demonstrates that he was exactly what Robert Greene said he was (see Chapter 3): an "upstart crow," an unprincipled bad actor who played a role that extended far beyond the proscenium stage. In other words, a farmer-turned theatrical entrepreneur, who made more than hay while the sun shone.

Mark Twain lived before the onset of the Age of Hollywood, or he would have understood immediately what was going on back then at the beginning of the Renaissance in England, which was simply the playing out of an exceptionally successful career by a businessman operating in accordance with the standard business practices of his particular field of endeavor (producing plays, which would nowadays translate into motion pictures). All of which was anathema to scholarly professors unaccustomed to detective work, let alone the business practices of producers, and comfortable only with such research as could be done in the safety of their ivory towers: detailed literary analysis of word usage and meter, theme and content, and so forth.

Shakespeare's authorship was accepted as a given. Alas, any dreams of finding proof beyond a name on the title page long after production had run its course—such things as hand-written manuscripts and lettered journals, the usual artifacts of a literary career remain unrequited, because none existed in the case of Shakespeare, and therefore had to be "surmised."

But stay—Shakespeare didn't operate in a scholarly vacuum. We don't know very much about him despite Lee's assertions, but what we do know confirms that he was one sharp operator. And as in Hollywood, the Elizabethan Theater was a business in which "property" (play) ownership was determined by such factors as possession, access, power, money, and clout, and had nothing to do with ascribing credits to the person or persons who actually put the original words on a piece of paper. As to the basic question that has most plagued the open-minded ever since Coleridge and Bright first doubted Shakespeare: If Shakespeare didn't write the plays, then who did? Indeed, the lack of a viable alternative candidate for the true authorship of the Works is the prime reason Shakespeare's stature persists, and may be the greatest example in history, aside from the conquest of the Americas, of possession being nine-tenths of the law.

Over the centuries doubters have submitted all sorts of candidates for the authorship, some frivolously, and others backed by all the power and zeal of a Taliban Committee, such as Edward de Vere (whose claims, as presented in the recent motion picture *Anonymous* I will address in chapter 8). At the time Mark Twain wrote his essay *Is Shakespeare Dead*? (which, notably, he only allowed to be published in his post-mortem autobiography) most skeptics, seeking a viable alternative to Shakespeare, turned to Sir Frances Bacon. Twain admitted he didn't know the answer himself, only that it certainly wasn't the man from Stratford.

Here's more from Mark Twain:

We will suppose a case: take a lap-bred, house-fed, uneducated, inexperienced kitten; take a rugged . . . Tom that's scarred from stem to rudder- post with the memorials of strenuous experience, and is so cultured, so educated, so limitlessly erudite that one may say of him "all cat-knowledge is his province"; also take a mouse. Lock the three up in a hopeless, crackless, exitless prison-cell. Wait half an hour, then open the cell, introduce a Shakespearite and a Baconian, and let them cipher and assume. The mouse is missing: the question to be decided is, where it is? You can guess both verdicts beforehand. One verdict will say the kitten contains the mouse; the other will as certainly say the mouse is in the tom-cat.

The Shakespearite will Reason like this—(that is not my word, it is his). He will say the kitten may have been attending school when nobody was noticing; therefore we are warranted in assuming that it did so; also, it could have been training in a court-clerk's office when no one was noticing, since that could have happened, we are justified in assuming that it did happen; it could have studied catology in a garret when no one was noticing—therefore it did; it could have attended cat-assizes on the shed-roof nights, for recreation, when no one was noticing, and have harvested a knowledge of cat court-forms and cat lawyer-talk in that way: it could have done it, therefore without a doubt it did; it could have gone soldiering with a war-tribe when no one was noticing, and learned soldier-wiles and soldier-ways, and what to do with a mouse when opportunity offers; the plain inference, therefore, is that this is what it did. Since all these manifold things could have occurred, we have every right to believe they did occur. These patiently and painstakingly accumulated vast acquirements and competence needed but one thing more—opportunity—to convert themselves into triumphant action. The opportunity came, we have the result; beyond a shadow of question the mouse is in the kitten.

Mark Twain may have named the wrong tomcat, and Shakespeare was no kitten, but his point is valid: for the Western literary world, blindness has proven more satisfying than vision.

Chapter Two

The Education of Will Shakspur

Write what you know. It's a basic maxim of Writing 101. And if so, no one ever made more of a mockery of said maxim than William Shakespeare, if he was the man the facts confirm him to be: an uneducated agrarian theatrical entrepreneur from Stratford-on-Avon in rural Warwickshire, England. Based on the available evidence, this man knew lots of things: how to manipulate malt supplies, hoard grain to drive up the price, make loans, pawn costumes, stable horses, perform bit parts, and somehow acquire plays. But he never thought to write anything (let alone plays) on those subjects. He never used his Warwickshire homeland for the setting of any of the English plays, oddly preferring Marlowe's Kent, instead. Nor did he have any known access to or knowledge of the subjects he supposedly *did* write about.

Far be it for me to suggest he wasn't clever, of course. In the manner of, say, P.T. Barnum, he must have been very clever indeed, and possibly a genius. Just not at writing.

In that erudite stone-cut epitaph on Shakespeare's tomb, several words are misspelled. Shakespeare's defenders insist that the spelling errors are attributed to the illiteracy of the stone cutter—a plausible argument. But that fails to explain the juvenile and superstitious choice of words—the words of an illiterate man. It also confirms and emphasizes the illiteracy of Shakespeare's own heirs.

They, after all, had to approve that cheesy stone-cutting. Apparently, they liked it just fine. It evidently never occurred to them to at least mention the Bard's alleged career and accomplishments, not even in passing.

The true author of Shakespeare's Canon possessed, as any reader or playgoer knows, intimate knowledge of ancient Greece, Rome, Renaissance Italy, the French, Greek, and Latin languages and cultures, as well as the best and most creative comprehension of the English language ever held by one man. He had an unprecedented vocabulary: the largest of anyone who ever lived, more than double the 8,000 words employed by Milton in his works. He somehow acquired a comprehensive knowledge of English history, of law and medicine, a full understanding of the art of poetry, of philosophy, of the interaction between social classes, of the use of comedy, of tragedy, and all the inner workings of the human soul. All with no education or life experience anyone knows of. Not bad for a guy who owned no books! Maybe he had a tutor, or picked up a few pointers on the side from Marlowe, like he did in *Shakespeare in Love*, or like the super-powered ingenue in the film *Crouching Tiger, Hidden Dragon.* This between harvests, in a small farm town far from any center of learning or culture. But then, who are we to doubt a deity?

Remarkably, Shakespeare's supporters not only insist this is so, but refuse to consider any alternative. Still, with all that brilliance, one would think he'd at least have wanted to write a letter or two, maybe take a couple of trips, to actually see some of those places he wrote so effusively about. And maybe take his children along with him. Or at least teach them to read!

As any college graduate student knows, in academia, budding scholars are dependent on close relationships with their professors and mentors, who maintain strict requirements in terms of areas of study, and rigorous control over degree programs and credentials. In order to earn a doctorate in English Literature and its requisite knowledge of Shakespeare, it's not advisable to march into your faculty advisor's office and announce you're going to challenge his life's work. Trust me, I've tried. In academe, like in church, one is expected to accept existing doctrine without question. The strange thing is, by their own admission, no academic ever had a hand in the immaculate Shakespearean education. Instead, we are obliged to believe he somehow acquired all that education *despite* being born, raised, and living out most of his life as an agrarian merchant in a town that had no library and no access to books, and whose one elementary school there is no evidence he ever attended. If conclusions were based strictly on facts, an inquiring investigator might wonder that, unlike virtually all other Elizabethan playwrights, *there is no record of William Shakespeare having ever attended any school at all.* Far from being curious about the outside world, the young Will Shakespeare was content to stay at home flaying sheep and entertaining milk maids until unwanted domestic responsibilities and the threat of punishment for petty crimes apparently drove him to flee to London. Nor did he ever feel the need to study abroad, or study at all!

Perhaps he was home-schooled. By his illiterate parents, apparently. No matter. Yet again, Shakespeare's defenders insist we accept this minor anomaly without question.

Shakespearean scholars, while dismissing all this skepticism as being much ado about nothing, have had more trouble explaining why no one *else* in Shakespeare's family ever acquired an education of any sort either, including his own wife and children. Surely such a literate papa as our William would have inspired at least a smidgen of book learning amongst his brood. Even if he was a Rolling Stone. But no.

Maybe he was too busy. Yet it's not as though he was away all the time like an itinerant mariner or foreign legionnaire. Shakespeare spent most of his life right at home, pursuing non-theatrical business ventures in rural Stratford, England. By choice. And after ten years of hiatus on the London theater circuit, returned there a rich man. Yet even with all that supposed accumulation of wisdom, knowledge and experience under his belt, he *still* didn't share any of it with his family. Maybe they weren't interested. Perhaps they dismissed him as a geek, poor chap. That could explain why his many recorded possessions, at the time of his death, didn't include one single book. But then, our kids don't read much either, these days. Maybe he was a visionary after all: a man of his time, and ours.

As to Shakespeare's failure to educate his son, this omission by a presumably literary man aspiring to a higher social station (having acquired land and wealth of his own) is somewhat puzzling. Perhaps he intended to home school the boy himself. After he was finished brokering costumes, making loans, hoarding grains, and acquiring real estate. But this minor oversight too, like the Bard's own lack of education, is blithely dismissed by the Shakespeareans as unimportant.

Staunch Shakespeare defender Irwin Leigh Matus (*Shakespeare, in Fact*) excuses Shakespeare's lack of schooling as being due to inadequate record keeping. Some sort of a bureaucratic oversight, no doubt. Yet records were painstakingly kept in 16th-century England. Each of Shakespeare's land acquisitions, loans, lawsuits and payments is carefully recorded for posterity. Only the records of his education and literary activities seem to have been misplaced. Presumably, nobody was interested in those. Matus points out that there was no "record" of Ben Jonson having attended the famed Westminster School, either.

Perhaps when Jonson wrote of Westminster headmaster William Camden *"Camden most reverend head to whom I owe/All that I am in arts, all that I know,"* he was just being metaphorical. But then no one has questioned whether or not Ben Jonson attended Westminster, was really a writer, or had an education. Ben Jonson, like Christopher Marlowe and the other writers of the time, left a personal written record illustrative of his accomplishments. Jonson participated in the literary circles of his time, wrote extensive correspondence, and made specific dedications and acknowledgments (truthful or not) that can be traced to persons provably known to him. That's what writers did, and do. Except Shakespeare, it seems. Of course, one can hardly blame him for his lack of correspondence, if it's true, as some scholars frettingly suggest, that he could neither read nor write. It would have been very time-consuming and painstaking, after all, dictating missives and making journal entries with that excruciating scrawl of his. Yet again, as they say, 'genius will find away.'

Other Shakespeareans ford this torrent of doubt with the usual surmise: that Shakespeare "must have been" a student at the King's New (elementary) School at Stratford, as though that should settle the question. Cartographer and biographer Charles Hamilton is more circumspect. Beneath an illustration of the school on page 14 of his book *In Search of Shakespeare,* he inscribes: "Shakespeare may have been a student here." Or not.

Regarding the matter of the world's greatest literary figure not bothering to educate his children, akin to opera star Placido Domingo not bothering to teach his children a few basic tunes, Matus also takes pains to point out that for a man to fail to educate his daughters was "in keeping with the custom of the day." No doubt true, for rural farmers and businessmen. But one might think that a man of letters capable of writing a play like *The Tempest*, in which a father, Prospero, raises his daughter Miranda, as a lettered woman, even while in exile on an island, would have differing views. Unless, of course, he merely feigned all that depth, sensitivity, human understanding and wisdom when he wrote *Hamlet*, *King Lear*, *As You Like It* and those thirty three other incomparable treatises on the deepest, most intricate and complex of human thoughts, feelings, and behavior. Possibly deep down, he was just shallow. Kind of like Jack Nicholson's character in *As Good As it Gets*. Are we to hold that against him? Is it so hard to believe, as Shakespeareans insist, that the author who created Prospero and Miranda might simply have had more important things to do than to read to his own giftless daughters, or teach them to read? Or to encourage them to write themselves—poetry at least!— and achieve a higher position in life than just that of being another tradesman's housekeeper and cook? After all, it wasn't "common practice!" Judging from the available facts, Will Shakespeare was nothing, if not "common." Egalitarians everywhere might well rejoice in the knowledge that the real Shakespeare was just a conventional philistine like the rest of us, after all. But an inquiring mind, upon being asked to believe that the man who wrote *A Midsummer Night's Dream* and *The Taming of the Shrew* was so conventional, so custom driven, so oblivious to the wants and needs of the women in his own household as that, might have a few questions of his or her own. Because this sort of familial negligence does seem antithetical to common sense, not to mention the thematic content of the plays themselves. Perhaps he was just tired, from all the effort he apparently expended in order to educate himself. Like a weary commuter father, by the time he got back to the farm house, all he had energy for was dinner and a flagon of ale by the fire. Children should be seen, not heard. And after all, somebody has to cook and clean up.

But stay! While it might not take a classical education to write a frivolous farce or melodrama, our man Shakespeare is supposed to have written the greatest body of literary works ever composed. Even in these times of open popular antagonism towards those with higher education, can this really be possible? Well, to be fair, Hollywood has shown us again and again that you can do a lot with smoke and mirrors. Still, Shakespeare's supporters require us to believe that the Bard applied these skills with raw talent alone, and acquired them by hanging around the Green Room at the local theater, or the Queen's parlor or perhaps the Earl of Southampton's kitchen. Not that there's any evidence of this—but then, the basic building blocks for such literacy certainly weren't available in the farming town of Stratford-on-Avon, and again, there's no evidence he went anywhere else, including Southampton. Another common argument in academic circles is that only a little basic knowledge was needed, to write the plays. A third grader's knowledge, to be exact, since that's the farthest he could have gotten, in Stratford. A touch of medicine, a tad of law, a dab of Greek, a dash of genius and voila: art!

Of course, today there are plenty of successful writers who know nothing. Hollywood, one might suspect, is full of them. Some of whom, like Shakespeare, have made a pile of money. But (a) most of them actually wrote those scripts, and (b) no one, least of all they themselves, would dare suggest that their output be counted among the greatest literary achievements of all time. It is also true that there have always been competent writers sufficiently able to acquire adequate knowledge in fields other than their own to write about them.

Any fiction author today will confirm that a writer on many topics cannot possibly be an expert in all of them. Patricia Cornwell, one of the most popular and successful writers of the North American mystery genre, writes a series of novels featuring a medical examiner named Kate Scarpetta. Patricia Cornwell's books are entertaining, and convincing in their detail. Yet she is not a trained forensic pathologist, nor a medical examiner. Or any kind of doctor at all. She is simply a good writer who does research, hangs around the coroner's office, and takes notes. She's also known to her colleagues as a person who actually puts pen to paper. Unlike, say, Shakespeare.

Shakespearean scholars, including Matus, have acknowledged that certain scenes in *Henry V, Titus Andronicus* and *The Comedy of Errors* might have been composed with the collaboration of another colleague who was versed in those languages, which was common practice in a working theatrical company such as the King's Men. Those plays or scenes may even, some have dared to admit, have been entirely written by another.

Matus also insists, allowing the assumption that Will did indeed attend the local Stratford elementary school, that such schooling would in fact have provided adequate proficiency in Latin and history to provide the necessary interest and basic background to be a writer of sorts. This, of course, is possible, if one is writing, say, comic books. One would have to agree, as well, that such schooling would also allow him sufficient literacy to be a play-book prompter and indeed, a player, which he was (you have to be able to read your lines, after all!).

This version of events, however, would still leave a lot of explaining to do, as to how or where he acquired such a decidedly post-primary school vocabulary, knowledge of European and Grecian culture and history, and all those other trades and professions to boot.

As for worldly experience and access to knowledge in general, the prescribed supposition is that this came as a natural result of being on the theater circuit. This is like suggesting that attendance at numerous baseball games will make you a stellar center fielder.

Undaunted, Shakespeare defender Matus, determined to win the day, resorts to hearsay and analogy: a glowing tribute to an instructor at the Stratford Grammar School that Shakespeare *might have attended*, and a poorly worded quote in Latin from another boy who definitely did attend that school (*his* records weren't lost, as luck would have it), suggesting that such a testimonial proved the Stratford school more than adequate to provide all the education in Latin necessary to become a fine writer. From which we are obliged to conclude that Shakespeare gleaned enough from this level of education to have gone on from those hallowed rustic halls to write his histories, presumably forthwith!

As a point of interest, the boy who penned the above-mentioned letter was the son of a certain Richard Quiney—the one who wrote a wheedling letter to Shakespeare, a known moneylender, asking for a loan. The Quiney boy, incidentally, did not go on to write great works of his own (although he did marry Shakespeare's daughter Judith). Unless, of course, he used a pseudonym. As to this, for those who have suggested that W. Shakespeare was a front or pseudonym for another writer, this author respectfully suggests that surely they could have found a better candidate than young Mr. Quiney's moneylender. This Quiney letter, incidentally, as Mark Twain reported, is the only letter of any sort ever found among Shakespeare's personal records, archives or belongings (which, we mustn't forget, didn't include books either—at least he was consistent.) As to Shakespeare's not owning any books, the conventional explanation is that as an actor Shakespeare would have been invited to the homes and houses of the great lords of the time, presumably with ample opportunity to read all of *their* books (and take copious notes in his infamous scrawl), between tea and performances. Not that there is any evidence of this, or that any such notes exist. Nor is there need to explain how he learned enough to get invited to the party in the first place. The great universities might as well close down operations, if an illiterate backwoods glover/butcher's son can accomplish all this with no instruction, guidance or any input whatsoever from the denizens of Academe.

In summation, a diligent detective, investigating this interesting theory of self-education back in Elizabethan times, might experience considerable bafflement in trying to determine how he did it with neither schooling *nor* books. If he used smoke and mirrors, what kind of smoke? And where are the mirrors? But then, who are we, mere mortals, to question a deity? It's a wearisome, thankless task.

Shakespeare's defenders are limitless in their inventiveness and resourcefulness. Take their explanation for his legal knowledge, for example: that he "no doubt" served as an apprentice, at one time or another, to a lawyer. Never mind the awkward fact that in order to apprentice with a lawyer, one would have needed at least a bachelor's degree, then as now. But no matter. Where there's smoke, perhaps there's mirrors after all.

Let us give Shakespeare the benefit of the doubt, and allow that he "may have" gone to the local Stratford elementary school, and may even have taken Latin I (although there is no evidence of this). What is *not* in doubt is that he had no higher education whatsoever. And again, it's one thing to write popular pulp or movie fiction with a few basic facts one can cobble together from one or two good sources, like Holinshed. It's another thing altogether to write profoundly thoughtful, factual, historical or legal drama without some semblance of learning, whatever his followers might profess. Which is why today's best-selling fiction about doctors and lawyers tends to be written by, well, doctors (Robin Cook) and lawyers (Scott Turow and John Grisham). Shakespeare's defenders, many of whom are renowned, illustrious scholars with numerous impressive degrees from outstanding institutions (unlike their beloved Bard), seem unfazed by the notion that this man, this small-time actor and businessman, somehow educated himself to such a degree as to wildly surpass their own lofty achievements. Genius will find a way, we are instructed to believe, and that's that. And Academe has held the reigns of this doctrine with a grip tighter than that of a Roman charioteer since the paucity of biographical evidence first became apparent, a half century after the death of "The Bard."

ARTIST? OR CON ARTIST?

An artist can paint from sheer inspiration, without a shred of schooling or training. Take Jackson Pollock. Please. It's called *talent,* whatever we may think of the results. Pierre Gauguin had it, quit his stockbroker job at age 35 and moved to the South Pacific, where he made art history painting beautiful, scantily clad native girls and got a novel written about him. But that wouldn't work for a writer. A writer needs to know, for example, how to write. And while genius helps, it also requires some basic skills and training in the craft of wordsmanship. Never mind knowledge or experience relevant to the subject matter.

Once again, we are told, genius will find a way. Yet there is no other parallel in the history of genius. Mozart was meticulously tutored by his father, an accomplished musician and composer in his own right. Bach, Beethoven, Brahms, all were highly learned men. There never was a great composer who didn't study for years, and master not only composition but an instrument as well (usually the piano) or even multiple instruments, like Bach. Some great painters were self-taught, such as Van Gogh (after his dreadful potato-eaters period). But he, like all gifted souls, sought out other artists to work with, learn from, and emulate. Shakespeare, apparently, felt no need to do anything of the sort. Like a modern fifteen- year old, he already knew it all. All the other poets and playwrights of Elizabethan England were members of a small group of gifted, educated men (led by the so-called Cambridge University Wits) well known to the public and to each other. And yet our intrepid Bard, although working in the same city at the same time, didn't seem to feel the need to associate with the other writers in any way whatsoever. Maybe he was too good for them. In any case, he was never known to have been one of them, or even known any of them in any capacity, other than as a part-time actor and entrepreneur.

As of 1592, when Marlowe was at his zenith, the only thing Will Shakespeare was known as, in the theater business, was horse groomer. That is, until he got on the bad side of Oxford playwright Robert Greene, which we'll get into in the next chapter.

In summation, a moderately competent detective such as Alan Grant (fictional or otherwise), were he or she to look, would find no credible evidence whatsoever that William Shakespeare of Stratford-on-Avon, a humble man by birth and known in his own time only for some often quibbling and dubious business dealings, did, in fact, write a thing. William Shaksper/Shake-scene/Shakspeare may indeed have strutted and fretted his hour upon the stage, but never before or since in history has that kind of Tonypandy led to deification. It comes down to a simple, fundamental question, around which all sorts of scenarios of crime and conspiracy can be woven, which is this: how (other than through political intrigue tantamount to piracy and plagiarism or worse) could such a dubious and unqualified person become elevated to such immortality, from virtually out of the blue?

Which leads to a second, and equally compelling question, which is this: *at whose expense did he or his sponsors pull this off?*

Chapter Three

The 'Upstart Crow'

Were a latter-day investigator such as Tey's Alan Grant to examine the record, he would find that the first indication William Shakespeare even existed in the literary and theatrical circles of Elizabethan London, according to his own chroniclers, was that fierce invective directed against him by poet and playwright Robert Greene in 1592. In his Chaucer-esque pamphlet *A Groatsworth of Wit* Greene referred to an unknown "upstart crow, beautified with our feathers," and described him as considering himself "in his own conceit the only Shake-scene in the country."

No doubt this pamphlet lends itself to interpretation. Especially of the selective kind. The *Groatsworth* story itself is a parable about two brothers: one a businessman, the other a "scholler." On their father's death-bed the former is given all the assets except a single "groat," with which the scholar son is asked to acquire at least that amount's worth of wit, presumably because he has none. Predictably, it's the "better" brother who squanders the money, with the complicity of a "madam." A witless attempt at revenge backfires, leaving both brothers bereft. At this moment of discovery, the "Player" (Shake-scene) turns up:

You are a scholler, and pittie it is men of learning should live in lacke, he begins. The brother Roberto (guess who?) then asks how he might be employed. *Why, easily, quoth hee, and greatly to your benefit: for men of my profession get by schollers their whole living.* In other words, the broker makes his living exploiting scholars (read: writers).

What is your profession? asks Roberto. *Truely sir said he, i am a player*. The Player (Shake-scene) then describes how he is *a substantiall man, able to afford at my proper cost, to build a Windmill*. (According to his self-alleged illegitimate son, Sir William Davenant, Shakespeare did indeed boast of building a windmill once, perhaps in case Cervantes should come to visit). He goes on: *What though the worlde once went hard with mee, when I was faine to carrie my playing Fardle a footebacke*; explaining that he'd once been a poor puppeteer, but is better off now; *for my very share in playing apparrell will not be solde for two hundred pounds*. In other words, he's made money dealing in costumes, which he's not about to let go of. Robert questions him further, to which the Player enumerates his credentials:

I am as famous for Delphrigus, and the king of Fairies, as ever was any of my time. The twelve labors of Hercules have I terribly thundered on the stage, and placed three scenes of the devill on the highway to heaven. He then boasts that *I can serve to make a prettie speech, for I was a countrie Author, passing at a morall, for it was I that pende the Moral of mans wit, the Dialogue of Dives, and for seaven yeeres space was absolute interpreter of the puppets*.

As proof, he recites:

"The people make no estimation,
Of Morrals teaching education."

(Quick cut to the aforementioned famous Shakespeare epitaph for a similar spine-chilling reminder of this man's real talent!)

Then, like a wheedling neophyte seeking praise, the player pleads:

Was not this prettie for a plaine rime extempore? If ye will ye shall have more. Nay it is enough, said Roberto, but how meane you to use mee? Why sir, in making playes, said the other, for which you shall be well paied, if you will take the paines.

In other words, Trust me, good sir. Give me your plays (or write some for me) and I'll make you rich. Or at least, buy you lunch.

And so the player/broker solicits the works of a struggling playwright, promising financial reward: the daily pipe dream of your average Los Angeles wait person. It's pretty clear this *player* (ironically the same term is used in Hollywood today to describe a successful industry hustler, as opposed to actor) imagines himself a writer of sorts, who is also a pawnbroker, a former puppeteer and "extempore" of doggerel.

Greene names him later: Will Shake-scene, "Johannes factotum," who would prove to be the bane of said Robert Greene. It's interesting to note Greene's reference to the brokering of costumes, inasmuch as a large cache of them turned up decades later in Shakespeare's will (see Chapter 7). While such types abound in Hollywood today, no one else in known Elizabethan lore fit this description. Only William Shakespeare, poet-extempore.

Here is the famed passage from *Groatsworth* (the bold typeface is mine):

Base minded all three of you if by my misery you be not warned; for unto none of you, like me, sought these Burres to cleave; those Puppets, I mean, that speak from our mouths those Anticks garnished in our colours. Is it not strange that I, to whom they all have been beholden; is it not strange that you to whom they all have been beholden, shall, were you in that case I am now, be at once of them forsaken? Yes, trust them not; for there is an **upstart Crow, beautified with our Feathers**, *that,* **with his Tygers heart wrapped in a Players hide**, *supposes he is as well able to bombast out a blank verse as the best of you; and being an absolute* Johannes Factotum *is in his own conceit the only* Shake-scene *in a country, O that I might entreat you rare wits to be employed in more profitable courses and let those Apes imitate your past excellence and never more acquaint them with your admired inventions. I know the best husband of you all will never prooue a* Userer . . . *yet whilst you may seeke you better Maisters; for it is pittie men of such rare* wits, *should be subiect to the pleasures of such rude* ***groomes****.*

Greene mentions that this "Tyger's heart wrapped in a player's hide" supposes himself as being able to "bombast out a blank verse with the best of you," much as young Will Shakspur was said to have done in his father's butcher shop. That's all the Shakespeareans had or needed as proof of authorship, conveniently disregarding the rest of the piece completely. An inquiring mind might well wonder what "bombast" has to do with poetry or playwrighting. I suppose a player, particularly a boastful one who imagines himself to be a "poet extempore," might have a tendency towards "bombast." Especially after quaffing an ale or two at the Cheapside Inn. Maybe Jerry Falwell writes poems, too, on the side. Reciting doggerel while chopping mutton, however, does not necessarily a poet make. And even if he *was* bombasting blank verse, there's still no evidence he wrote any of it.

Now let's take a look at those descriptive terms and phrases underlined in the Greene text: "Puppets," "anticks," "feathers," "wits," "player," "Johannes factotum," "usurer" and "groomes." All synonymous, presumably, with "Bard." The 'upstart crow' is a reference to the famous Aesop fable *The Jackdaw and the Birds*, in which a jackdaw (or crow) beautifies himself with the feathers of other birds, in hopes of becoming King of the Birds. The "feathers" are the works of the writers (Greene himself, Kit Marlowe and the others).

Shakespeare, the "upstart crow," is the professional plagiarist (meaning "rival playwright of superior talent," we're told), agent/broker, and "factotum" who enriches ("beautifies") himself with said feathers (also a pun for their writing quills). In other words, a producer! The term "wits" almost certainly refers to the University Wits, who were the *known* writers of the time in London.

The metaphor of the crow "beautifying" himself with "our feathers" is also a pretty good description of a costume broker getting rich from brokering the accouterments of others. "Johannes factotum" translates not only to "jack of all trades," but also "Jack" as in "jackdaw," a European crow notorious for being a thief. So one of Greene's most significant charges was that Shake-scene was a broker: earlier on of costumes, then of plays, first on behalf of the Admiral's Men and later on the Chamberlain's Men (the two preeminent theater companies of his time). The term broker deserves special attention here. In Shakespeare's day as today, "broker" meant not just pawn broker, or costume broker, but one who dealt in property in general.

One form of "property"—in fact the principal form of property with which someone in Shakespeare's position dealt (in management of a major theatrical company) was the play itself. A play-broker (or agent) bought or otherwise acquired plays. It would be difficult to distinguish between an Elizabethan "play broker" and a modern Hollywood producer, aside from the vehicles they rode in and toys they played with. While Shakespeare was called an "agent," that had a different connotation in Elizabethan times. He wasn't selling plays to the studio, as today's agents would do. He was acquiring plays on behalf of his employers who later became his partners, which is what a producer, or even more precisely, a studio executive would do. And incidentally, very few of today (or yesterday's) film producers could resist at least a pretense at writing ("poetry extempore" perhaps? Or quaint epitaphs).

Or re-writing, as Shakespeare also claimed to have done (Greene's *Locrine* among others).

In those days, like in the early days of Hollywood, the buyer became the owner, and the owner could do as he pleased. It is clear that Robert Greene was, at the very least, accusing Shake-scene of bad faith in that capacity, which might explain why Shakespeare's name was on nearly as many bad plays as great ones (see Foul Plays for more). Greene was clearly implying that Shake-scene had commissioned one or more plays from him, possibly including parts of *Henry VI (Part I),* which the late Harvard lecturer and Elizabethan scholar Alden Brooks, Shakespeare biographer E.K. Chambers, and other scholarly dons have acknowledged was probably a collaboration of Greene and Marlowe, and the origin of the "tiger's heart" line. It was during that time that Shakespeare also acquired *Locrine*, registering it and claiming it for himself in 1594, after Greene was dead. The broker's refusal to pay him might have had something to do with Greene's bitter death-bed diatribe. Or maybe he was just having a bad day.

Harvard's Alden Brooks believed that the other three playwrights Greene was appealing to in *Groatsworth*—Marlowe, Nashe and probably Peele—were all working for Shakespeare by then, providing plays for the Chamberlain's Men on a commission basis.

Greene was warning them that they, like him, were going to get ripped off. Those guys would have felt right at home in Hollywood, alongside Faulkner and Fitzgerald.

The term **Puppet** is in reference to the little-cited earlier section of *Groatsworth* in which Greene's protagonist meets the actor-broker out in the countryside (from whence Shakespeare himself came, possibly with the Sheriff of Warwickshire hot on his trail for poaching.). It is this Shake-scene who reveals his earlier career as a puppeteer. As to some biographers' assertions that Greene must have been referring to some other player (Robert Wilson is often cited) this is like suggesting they must be talking about some other Shakespeare, because the entire parable in Groatsworth was clearly about one person. And, as Alden Brooks commented in his own book, William Shakespeare was the only known person at that time who was known as a player *and* claimed to be an author, beginning the week after Marlowe was presumed dead. (As to the latter, we'll deal with the merits of his writing later on).

Greene's "Shake-scene" was also a **usurer**. That too, is a serious indictment, about which our mischievous mole will dig up more dirt later. But Greene's absolute contempt for Shakespeare was broad and chilling, and pretty hard to ignore. Unless, of course, you're an English professor. Greene might have been all wet, in branding Shake-scene as the factotum of all factotums, or in modern terms, the P.T. Barnum of Warwickshire or the Sam Goldwyn of Bankside (or at least, the Globe Theater). Clearly he had a grudge. But be that as it may, his charges bore weight. He saw Shakespeare as being an unscrupulous merchant, bent on taking over the theater business, which is pretty much what he went on to do. Just because Greene was paranoid doesn't mean Shakespeare wasn't out to get him (or steal his plays, anyway).

Groome is a particularly interesting term which further identifies Shakespeare as the target of this invective, if further proof is needed. One of the few actual witnesses used by the Stratford proponents in piecing together their version of literary Tonypandy was the aforementioned Sir William Davenant, an actor whose father owned a pub in Oxford in those years, and who later claimed to be Shakespeare's illegitimate son. According to Davenant, Shakespeare was accustomed to stopping by the family establishment regularly to imbibe during his trips home to Stratford. And mess with the barmaids, it seems. It was Davenant who provided the story that Shakespeare was the Elizabethan equivalent of a Hollywood theater car-park valet in his early days in London. For those who don't read Dick Francis or go to the races, a horse-handler is known as a groom.

Biographer Nicholas Rowe quoted a contemporary named Dowdall who reported that Shakespeare had first entered the theater "in servitude," or as Rowe himself put it, "very low ranke." This is consistent with Greene's "rude groomes" and Sir William Davenant's story about Shakespeare starting out as a livery man, which business continued right up until Henry Burbage was forced to move the theaters across the Thames. After which London theatergoers traveled by boat. John Aubrey, the Renaissance equivalent to gossip columnist Walter Winchell, referred to Davenant repeatedly. It was Aubrey who Shakespeareans cited for "proof" that young Shakespeare, while apprenticing in his father's butcher's shop in Stratford, was already a young man of literary prowess. According to Aubrey, "when he kill'd a calf he would doe it in a high style, and make a speech." Perhaps something pithy along the lines of *"The people make no estimation, Of Morrals teaching education."*

All of these charges by Greene are pretty interesting, because they establish Shakespeare's true scope of activities in the theater. Not one of them refers in any way to a budding playwright or for that matter play "doctor," as the Shakespeareans have long had us believe. Greene was clever. Like many a writer, he didn't want to just come out and name names, which might lead to such unpleasantness as, say, getting pounded in a back alley, or worse. He knew he risked counter-charges of being, say, a sore loser (which have been made anyway). So he applied his literary skills to metaphor and allusion, layering meaning upon meaning in his parable: plagiarist, usurer, groom, play broker, costume broker, thief, all were characteristics of his *Johannes factotum.*

Greene's writing is annoyingly allegorical at times, but his warning to his colleagues is clear enough. Let's take a look at the actual Fable to which he refers:

THE JACKDAW AND THE BIRDS

Wishing to establish a King of the Birds, Zeus set a date for summoning them all before him for comparison: he would choose the most beautiful to reign over them. The birds went off then to the shallow water near the shore of a river to wash. Now the jackdaw (crow) realizing his ugliness, went around gathering up the feathers from the other birds, which he then arranged and attached to his own body. Thus he became the most handsome of all. Then the big day arrived and all the birds presented themselves before Zeus. The jackdaw, with his motley adornment, was among them. And Zeus voted for him to be the royal bird on account of his beauty. But the other birds, outraged at this decision, each pulled out the feather that had come from him. The result was that the jackdaw was stripped and once again became just a jackdaw. Aesop

If only Greene's denouement had turned out the same way.

Scholars have had countless debates over the meaning of these words, with the Shakespeareans always twisting them in their favor, which is pretty mystifying. Some skeptics insist that "Shake-scene" was a colloquial metaphor of the time, probably equivalent to "Scene-stealer." Maybe. In any case, you'd think that since the Shakespeareans insist "Shake-scene" is their guy, they'd at least own up to what Greene had to say about him, whether he was Shakespeare, Shakspere, Shackspear or Shakspur (all used by the man at one time or another). Instead, they insist that Greene and others were merely jealous of "Shake-scene" for "rewriting" and "bettering" their plays.

Which is not exactly consistent with a jackdaw ripping off other people's feathers (in other words, masquerading as a playwright) while busy being a puppeteer, broker, actor (bombasting blank verse), usurer, and groome: a *Johannes Factotum*. In other words, a typical producer!

Maybe they thought no one would notice. Maybe they thought no one would care. Evidently they were right.

William Shakespeare, in 1592, had not yet been in any way recognized or heard of as a writer. That Shakespeare was known at all was due to his having positioned himself at the transom of one of the principle London playhouses, probably The Curtain, somehow making money. His name is mentioned in no other capacity besides "puppeteer," "broker," "player," "factotum" "usurer" and "groome" until a year later, in 1593. And then only by a post-publication "dedication" to the poem *Venus and Adonis* the significance of which I will discuss later in this book.

That Shakespeare was acquiring plays by that time is certain. He was clearly Greene's employer, then on behalf of Lord Strange's or Admiral's Men, taking scripts including the anonymously submitted *Locrine*, among others, and inscribing them with his own initials as having "overseen" and "corrected" (it remained pretty bad). But at that time there is no evidence he had written a farthing's worth of prose or poetry of his own. So Robert Greene was calling Shakespeare a lot of things, none of them complimentary, and none of them a writer.

Primarily a poet and essayist for most of his career, Robert Greene did in fact begin writing plays around the time Shakespeare first came to London (generally believed to be 1586), and like modern screenwriters who brave Hollywood, fared badly in the business deals therefrom. For which he blamed Shakespeare. In other words, Shakespeare, as producer, bought or otherwise acquired plays for the Company (read: *studio*). From Robert Greene among others, which might explain all those so-called "foul plays" that scholars with straight faces and stiff necks unblinkingly reject as having no place in Shakespeare's Canon. What they of course refuse to consider because it destroys their case, is that Shakespeare simply acquired plays for the Chamberlain's Men without discernment between good and bad, and later sold them off with his own name imprinted thereon, for further profit.

Shakespeare was also prime candidate for the "connycatcher" ("con-man") Greene derided so bitterly in yet another essay, the *Quip for an Upstart Courtier*, since he and "Shake-scene" are virtually identical in character, demeanor, style, and substance. Perhaps Greene meant some other puppeteer/player/userer/broker or groom in town. But Shakespeare seems to have recognized himself in that mirror, because he was furious with Greene for the following description of the player-broker in *Upstart Courtier*, which allegedly identifies Shakespeare with another similar Aesopian analogy: "*The peacocke wrapte in the pride of his beauteous fethers is knowne to be but a dunghill bird by his foul feete.* (sic)"

Hmmm. All those feathers again. Let's take a look, then, at a previously undiscussed passage in Greene's *Upstart Courtier* that sets the stage for his disparagement of Shakespeare as "agent." This same disparagement appears later in the Canon itself, in the form of Pandarus in *Troilus and Cressida*. Note the description:

. . . There was coming alongst the valley towards us a square set fellow, well fed and briskly appareled, in a black taffeta doublet and a spruce leather jerkin with crystal buttons, a cloak faced afore with velvet and a Coventry cap of the finest wool—his face something ruby bluish, cherry-cheeked, like a shred of scarlet or a little darker like the lees of old claret wine: a nose, autem nose, purpled preciously with pearl and stone like a counterfeit work. And between the filthy rheumicast of his blood-shotten snout there appeared small holes whereat worms' heads peeped as if they meant by their appearance to preach and show the antiquity and ancienty of his house. This fiery-faced churl had upon

his fingers as many gold rings as would furnish a goldsmith's shop, or beseem a pander of long profession to wear.

Wondering what companion this should be, I inquired of what occupation he was? Marry sir (quoth he) a broker—why do you ask?

Again, there is not a whole lot here to suggest a hidden literary genius. What Greene was describing is the Elizabethan equivalent of Victor Hugo's Thenardier (*Les Miserables*) whose sleazy and unprincipled depiction of a tradesman suited "Shake-scene" rather neatly.

Ignoring this, Shakespeareans seize upon another line in *Groatsworth* as further proof of Shakespeare's authorship: "*With his Tyger's heart wrapped in a Player's hide.*" This charge is serious indeed, because this line is clearly lifted from *Henry VI part III*: **"O, Tiger's heart, Wrapped in a woman's hide!"** which play Shakespeare chronologists believe was first staged between 1589 and 1592. What they tend to forget is that the play was registered and produced anonymously, first of all, and that Christopher Marlowe was the only known playwright in those years writing histories (again, Shakespeare was not known to be writing at all, other than doggerel). Most Shakespearean scholars, particularly J.M. Robertson and to a lesser extent E.K. Chambers, have grudgingly acknowledged that Shakespeare did not write "most of" this play, and that it was Marlowe, not Shakespeare, who wrote much or all of Parts *II* and *III* of *Henry VI*. In any case, at least in my experience the delivery of a line does not ownership make, any more than a name on a title page. The average Hollywood screenwriter would probably drop dead for joy if someone quoted a line from a movie he or she wrote, and actually acknowledged him or her as the author. Most viewers can't even name the writer, and don't care. Usually, they are "quoting" the actor who delivered the line.

("Didn't you just love it when Mel Gibson told Helen Bonham Carter 'Woman, get thee gone!'?") Another favorite is Arnold Schwartzenegger's insightful "Hasta la vista, Baby!" Gleaned, no doubt, from his extensive experience hanging out with all those Chicanos back home in Austria.

In an interview-review of Oprah Winfrey's movie *Beloved* the critic raved about a line Oprah delivers in this film, which she subsequently used to promote a new television show. The line was "You your best thing." Nowhere in the interview, nowhere in the review, does either the critic or Oprah herself mention who actually wrote the line. It became her line. Just as "make my day" became Clint Eastwood's line. Clint Eastwood probably doesn't even remember the true origin of his trademark quote. Why should he? And if Oprah knows who wrote her new trademark line, she didn't bother to say (the writing credits belonged to Toni Morrison and Akosua Busia). It's entirely possible Robert Greene couldn't have named the author of *Henry VI* in any case, since no one else did at the time. Nor was he trying to. He was parodying the posturing of a self-important and unscrupulous actor/broker and warning of his ill-intentions, which is what the entire missive was about.

Whether or not Shakespeare was any sort of writer at all such as he claimed to be to Greene (which requires us to ignore all that evidence suggesting that he was illiterate) Greene obviously didn't think much of the man's talent, and expressed that view in vehement terms. But Greene was more than contemptuous. He was fearful. *Groatsworth's* ominous portend is loud and clear. He is warning his friends to beware of this upstart, this faker, this usurper, this plagiarist, this thief. The warning is especially directed to Christopher Marlowe.

If only Marlowe had heeded him! Because judging by the outcome, he, like Greene, clearly delivered himself, his works, and his career directly into the jaws of the lion. Or in this case, "**tyger**."

Looking further, if all this isn't enough already, Greene as critic had few kind words to say about another play, *Fair Em*, that appeared in a book called *Shakespeare, Volume I*, from the collection of Charles I. This is another one of those "foul" plays that have proven a recurring embarrassment to the Shakespeareans. Shortly after Greene died, a printer named Thomas Creede published two plays: one anonymously, titled *Selimus*, then another, the aforementioned *Locrine*.

That Greene had sold plays to Shakespeare would be the probable cause of his outrage at getting stiffed, as expressed in *Groatsworth*, and one might therefore conclude that those plays were Greene's. *Fair Em* was highly forgettable, except that the role of William the Conqueror in this play was written (according to most scholars) especially for Shakespeare the player. Creede published a number of other plays of Greene's in 1594, many of which have been connected, in one way or another, to Shakespeare. Since the Admiral's Men with whom Shakespeare had been connected broke up that year, he could easily have purchased (or taken) the remaining plays and had them published himself, to make a little extra profit. The Admiral's Men had been going downhill for five years, since the ascendancy of the Chamberlain's players, which specialized in staging the plays of Christopher Marlowe, which were easily the best plays of the time, and suspiciously similar to a lot of the Bard's early works (OK, a lot of scholars argue otherwise, but we'll look at the plays themselves later on).

What is especially irritating about the Bard's biographers, going back to Nicholas Rowe, is their propensity for manipulating facts to suit predetermined conclusions. Sort of like a Florida election.

Thus a denunciation of a man with "*a tyger [predator]'s heart wrapped in a Player's [actor's] hide*" somehow, inexplicably, becomes a paean to an emerging literary genius. And yet aside from the name on *Venus and Adonis* (more on that later), the Quartos and Frances Meres' brief mention of some of the Works in his compilation of Elizabethan plays published in 1598 (*Palladis Tamia*), this is the only mention at all of Shakespeare's existence on the literary or theatrical scene *in his lifetime*.

The Shakespeareans require us to believe Robert Greene was merely jealous about Shakespeare being such a great writer, but Greene never once expressed jealousy. Rage, yes. Indignation, to be sure. Jealousy? Of what? Shakespeare was unknown as a writer at that time or any time in his lifetime.

Alden Brooks believed Greene had another grievance as well: abandonment. Greene was a burnout, and seemed to be of the opinion that our beloved Shakespeare had bled him dry, then dumped him. Greene's greatest complaint of all was that "Shake-scene" had left him in poverty, literally starving, a broken, dying man who would be dead within a month. It doesn't take a rocket scientist to conclude that Robert Greene was trying to warn his fellow writers about a non-writer who was pretending to be a writer, or a writer's rep, using their plays, making money from them, and enhancing his reputation with their works. In other words, a producer. Academe's conclusion? You're just jealous, baby!

What is particularly chilling about Greene's use of Aesop's fable, is its lack of resolution. If his charges were true, the man got away with it big time. To date, the crow (or at least his brand name) is still passing as a peacock, and remains adorned with his self-beautification. The London birds were never able to reclaim their feathers. Robert Greene's diatribe of 1592 was published a year before anything with Shakespeare's name on it officially appeared that anybody knows of. But in light of Shakespeare's later plagiarism (apparently forgivable in academic circles) such as the blatant theft of Marlowe's poem *The Passionate Shepherd* published under Shakespeare's name in *Passionate Pilgrim*, the "upstart crow" warning seems to have been chillingly prophetic.

Robert Greene died on September 3rd, 1592, two weeks before his grievances and warning to Marlowe and the other playwrights were published. Prior to his death he partook in a fatal "banquet" of Rhenish wine and pickled herring with Thomas Nashe, his and Marlowe's friend, and an unidentified stranger called Will Monox. The identity of this stranger remains a mystery, other than that, according to Nashe, he was a Player. Greene, already ill, died shortly afterwards of a bad stomachache. Alden Brooks, research biographer Louis Ule and others contend that Will "Monox" was Shakespeare, enraged by Greene's earlier description of him in *Quip for an Upstart Courtier*. Well, who knows? Maybe the Shadow knows . . .

Greene allegedly apologized for his outburst but by then it was too late. Nashe was quick to apologize to Shakespeare after Greene's death (perhaps wisely) and denied any support for Greene's opinions.

But Alden Brooks suggests that maybe this was because Nashe was also in the employ by then of "Shake-scene," and didn't want to lose his job. So by 1592 Will Shakespeare was a player in every sense, in the theater business. Based solely on Greene's vituperation, Shakespearean scholars cite that year as proof that Shakespeare was already a prominent writer. It mostly just indicates that he was a bad actor.

Shakespeare was clearly someone to be reckoned with: deeply involved in the theater business, who thought a lot of himself, and someone London's writers should be warned about, because he was a jackdaw or crow who liked to beautify himself with the "feathers" of others. In other words, a regular old-fashioned producer.

Chapter Four

The Man from Stratford

Shakespearean scholars, whenever challenged regarding the authorship, invariably trumpet the same old refrain: that there is more biographical material available on the Bard, more documentation on his life, more books and scholarly studies and detailed analyses of his work, than of any other author in history. This may be true. But as Sir George Greenwood pointed out, what they fail to mention is that not one word of all that literature, not one iota of that evidence, not one fragment in any way confirms that Shakespeare was a poet, playwright, or in any way at all a literary man.

Virtually the entire body of *biographical* knowledge about Shakespeare reveals an unscrupulous bit player and country businessman. Period. The "Elizabethan" town of Stratford itself is right out of the annals of P.T. Barnum. Or Walt Disney World. Or a Hollywood studio back lot. According to Alden Brooks, not one stick, not one stone of the pleasingly quaint tableau set forth for today's tourist trade existed in Shakespeare's time. The so-called "New Place" presented as his home was torn down twice before, in 1702 and 1759. It's "new" all right.

The famed Shakespeare bust in Stratford that originally depicted a crafty old man holding a bag of grain—Shakespeare's actual and only proven Stratfordian business enterprise—was redesigned forty years after his death by a draughtsman named Dugdale based on an alleged "death mask," then completely redesigned again a few years later with an entirely new face. This "beautification" was based on an idealized vision concocted by an early bardolotrist named Reverend Joseph

Greene in 1759. It was he who replaced the sack of grain with quill and scroll, clever fellow. Talk about a major rewrite (of history).

Interestingly, it was this same Reverend Greene (no relation to poor Robert) who also discovered Shakespeare's controversial will (see Chapter 7). Similar treatments were accorded the various "portraits" that have been generated over the centuries, as England rediscovered its forgotten "Bard" with enough versions of his alleged visage to populate Central Casting. Yet he wasn't remembered at all in Stratford, his hometown, until May of 1746, almost a hundred and fifty years after his death, when a strolling player named John Ward showed up, saw that there was money to be made, and established what would become the literary equivalent of Universal Studio Tours.

How did this happen, that an illiterate country butcher, bailiff and/or glovemaker's son (depending on who you choose to believe) should become credited with being the greatest writer of all time, without a scrap of evidence that either he or anyone else in his family before or after had so much as a single day of schooling, or ever set one word on paper other than a scrawled signature? And what about all those learned books and biographies, an entire Shakespeare library (the Folger Shakespeare Library in Washington, D.C.) dedicated to the scholarly study of the man and his works, if there is no substance to it?

We have always accepted Shakespeare's genius as a given. There are enormous and powerful institutions dedicated to this man, to his name, to his legacy. Stratford-on-Avon is the second biggest tourist attraction in the United Kingdom, reaping for the British economy untold billions over the centuries. The very language of our forebears is framed in Shakespeare's works. In his epistle to the First Folio of 1623 Ben Jonson called him "a man not of an age, but for all time!"

This was very nice, of course, in effect giving Shake-scene game, set, and match. No one seemed to notice or recall that Jonson had both doubted and ridiculed Shakespeare for his entire career, perhaps knowing more than he cared to say. This was the same Ben Jonson who decades earlier had said that Shakespeare (like his epitaph) "wanted (lacked) art." Clearly in the earlier case he was speaking of the man, the "factotum," and in the eulogy of the plays themselves. Lacked art? There's no certainty that Shakespeare could even sign his own name. He didn't bother on his wedding certificate. Of the six existing Shakespeare "signatures" no two match. The very spelling of the name varies in each, and all are the scrawl of a drunken farm hand, not a sophisticated scribe. To explain this away, the Stratford gang has been very inventive, surmising that he "must have had" palsy, among other afflictions, or that clerks always signed for him, because he was so busy. Good one. That might explain a shaky hand. Yet, unless one accepts the claims of some Stratford "scholars" that he wrote the will himself (an odd claim since its very content is so bumpkinesque, and marginally literate) there are no other specimens in existence of his writing.

A good detective, upon close scrutiny of the Shakespeare biographical material, would find the "evidence" of authorship as devoid of material substance as the emperor's proverbial wardrobe. All of those scholarly texts, in all those libraries, are a rich but synthetic tapestry covering up the startling dearth of plausible and verifiable facts. All of them are lavish with praise for the alleged tailor/poet's accouterments, articulating in splendid detail the fine texture of the cloth, the beauty of the weave, the intricacy of the décolletage, the perfection of the seam. All of it is couched in conclusive terms such as "we can easily deduce" and "readily construe," and "additionally infer."

The entire wardrobe, not just the suit, is risible: a construct based on assumption, supposition, speculation, conjecture, hypothesis, interpolation, theory, and mostly opinion. Alas, poor Yorick, they knew him not at all. The entire structure on which Shakespearean orthodoxy is built has no foundation whatsoever. It is all based on what Mark Twain calls *surmise.*

Unfortunately, we also know that True Believers are hardly dissuaded by mere facts. One of the most interesting facts about Shakespeare is the lack of elegy about his passing. Elegy was the most common method of tribute and recognition in Elizabethan times. Why would no one, not one person, acknowledge him in some way, with some tribute, however slight? How could it be that no one would lament the passing of such a great man? The only known mention at all of his death in 1616 was by his son-in-law, John Hall, who wrote in his journal: "My father-in-law died on Thursday." You can almost hear the yawns of ennui across the centuries. Nothing about his father-in-law the poet and playwright, the great author, the beloved Bard of Avon? One can't help but speculate about this, and make some suppositions as well. Such as the possibility that William Shakespeare wasn't acknowledged because he didn't write anything to acknowledge, that his name was on the quartos and Folio only because, like a movie producer who puts his name above the main title, he helped himself to the Works being sent or submitted to the Globe by another man living in exile.

While many have questioned, others doubted, and still others belittled the pedigree of William Shakespeare of Stratford-on-Avon, no one since George Greenwood has truly grappled with the unpleasant task of calling the emperor's attention to his naked condition. Lifetime doubter and author A. D. Wraight, as well as other English skeptics have all treated the glove-maker's son with kid gloves, making excuses for him, afraid to take on the vast Shakespearean institutional establishment and tourist trade. But if the skeptics were right, there is a strong possibility that crimes were committed, history was deliberately twisted, distorted, and falsified to benefit Mr. Shakespeare, and fortunes were made because of it. Including Shakespeare's own. Now that would be a crime of stupendous proportions.

There's also that small matter often mentioned by Shakespeare's biographers as harmless fun, the story of his having been a thief as a young man stealing deer from Sir Thomas Lucy's park in Stratford. This, like the horse grooming business, originates from the stories of Sir William Davenant, the same guy who claimed to be Shakespeare's illegitimate son. This deer-poaching anecdote was confirmed by early biographer Edward Capell among others. Once a thief, always a thief? Possibly prophetic tales aside, the notion that maybe, just maybe, Shakespeare was at best a front, if not a fraud, is not new in literary circles. This is where Mark Twain's pointed observation regarding supposition comes in once again, referring to Shakespeare's vast unexplained knowledge in so many fields of expertise:

How did he acquire these rich assets? In the usual way: by surmise.

Mark Twain had a lot more to say about Shakespeare as well:

How curious and interesting is the parallel—as far as the poverty of biographical details is concerned—between Satan and Shakespeare. It is wonderful, it is unique, it stands quite alone, there is nothing resembling it in history, nothing resembling it in romance, nothing approaching it even in tradition. How sublime is their position, and how over-topping, how sky-reaching, how supreme—the two Great Unknowns, the two Illustrious Conjecturabilities! They are the best-known unknown persons that have ever drawn breath upon the planet.

And further:

I *haven't any idea that Shakespeare will have to vacate his pedestal this side of the year 2209. Disbelief in him cannot come swiftly, disbelief in a healthy and deeply loved tar baby has never been known to disintegrate swiftly . . .*

He ought to have explained that he was . . . merely a nom de plume for another man to hide behind . . .

A willing front man, at best. A clever, unscrupulous entrepreneur doing business with a flair more likely, a blatant thief of another's creativity and recognition (financial and otherwise) at worst.

Consider this: Will Shakespeare appeared out of nowhere with no literary background or history whatsoever, with no known existence as an author when, in 1593, two weeks after his greatest and most likely rival for the true authorship vanished forever from the face of the Earth (we'll get to him shortly.) he published "his" first poem, *Venus and Adonis*, a poem which had previously been registered anonymously, with the Company of Stationers, the Elizabethan equivalent to the copyright office. Some scholars have suggested that Shakespeare may have lent or licensed his name as a sideline, which might explain the "foul plays" (all those bad ones with his name on them). Yet if his name was abused by being placed by others on the so-called "foul plays" Shakespeare never once objected, and gladly pocketed the proceeds. What would Tey's Alan Grant make of that?

That a man named William Shakespeare from Stratford-on-Avon existed, there is no question. That he was an actor (not a particularly notable actor, certainly no Edward Alleyn) is confirmed. As to the plays, had his name not suddenly, somehow, miraculously turned up on the Quartos and Folio, his authorship would never have been an issue. To even suggest such would have brought peals of scornful laughter from the very scholars who now so adamantly prop up his benighted edifice.

The problem is that Shakespeare is an industry, a Major Brand Name, and always was. Like Disney, Universal Studios, M.G.M., or Warner Brothers. I've already mentioned that his "sites" are collectively the second highest grossing tourist attractions in the United Kingdom. And for that reason alone, the British establishment will not stand down quietly, and will still insist in the most indignant and vociferous tones that indeed, the Titanic is in fine shape, the passengers are all well and happy, the ship's just been delayed a bit.

Now, thanks to the inevitable meddling of Hollywood and its motion picture sensation *Shakespeare in Love* two whole new myths have been fabricated—of Shakespeare the hero and lover, and the Earl of Oxford—a lifelong playboy—as an *Anonymous* genius. But a close look at any of the Shakespeare "portraits," a browse through any of his biographical histories, will uncloak anyone that even vaguely resembles that dashing image, or those roles. William Shakespeare, who had no problem ditching his wife and kids, was no hero. Or lover. He never even played one. Why, then, is it such a stretch to suggest that he wasn't a writer either? (More on Oxford elsewhere).

THE FACTS

All we really know of Shakespeare the man, all that is firmly documented in regards to his life prior to his sudden emergence onto the literary scene out of nowhere at the age of 30, Mark Twain described in the following brief biography (1909):

For the instruction of the ignorant I will make a list, now, of those details of Shakespeare's history which are facts—verified facts, established facts, undisputed facts.

FACTS:

He was born on the 23rd of April, 1564.

Of good farmer-class parents who could not read, could not write, could not sign their names.

At Stratford, a small back settlement which in that day was shabby and unclean, and densely illiterate. Of the nineteen important men charged with the government of the town, thirteen had to "make their mark" in attesting important documents, because they could not write their names.

Of the first eighteen years of his life, nothing is known. They are a blank.

On the 27th of November (1582) William Shakespeare took out a license to marry Anne Whateley.

Next day William Shakespeare took out a license to marry Anne Hathaway. She was eight years his senior.

William Shakespeare married Anne Hathaway. In a hurry. By grace of a reluctantly granted dispensation there was but one publication of the banns.

Within six months the first child was born.

About two (blank) years followed, during which period nothing at all happened to Shakespeare, so far as anybody knows.

Then came twins—1585. February.

Two blank years follow.

Then—1587—he makes a ten-year visit to London, leaving the family behind.

Five blank years follow. During this period nothing happened to him as far as anybody actually knows.

Then—1592—there is mention of him as an actor.

Next year—1593—his name appears on the official list of players.

Next year—1594—he played before the Queen. A detail of no consequence: other obscurities did it every year of the forty-five of her reign. And remained obscure.

Three pretty full years follow. Full of play-acting. Then: In 1597 he bought a New Place, Stratford.

Thirteen or fourteen busy years follow; years in which he accumulated money, and also a reputation as an actor and manager.

Meantime his name, liberally and variously spelt, had become associated with a number of great plays and poems, as (ostensibly) author of the same.

Some of these, in these years and later, were pirated, but he made no protest.

Then—1610-11—he returned to Stratford and settled down for good and all, and busied himself in lending money, trading in tithes, trading in land and houses; shirking a debt of forty-one shillings, borrowed by his wife during his long desertion of his family; suing debtors for shillings and coppers;

being sued himself for shillings and coppers; and acting as confederate to a neighbor who tried to rob the town of its rights in a certain common, and did not succeed.

He lived five or six years—till 1616—in the joy of these elevated pursuits. Then he made a will, and signed each of its three pages with his name.

It was a thoroughgoing business man's will. It named in minute detail every item of property he owned in the world—houses, lands, sword, silver-gilt bowl, and so-on—all the way down to his "second best bed" and its furniture.

It carefully and calculatingly distributed his riches among the members of his family, overlooking no individual of it. Not even his wife; the wife he had been enabled to marry in a hurry by urgent grace of a special dispensation before he was nineteen; the wife whom he had left husbandless so many years; the wife who had had to borrow forty-one shillings in her need, and which the lender was never able to collect of the prosperous husband, but died at last with the money still lacking. No, even this wife was remembered in Shakespeare's will.

He left her that "second-best bed."

And not another thing; not even a penny to bless her lucky widowhood with.

It was eminently and conspicuously a business man's will, not a poet's.

It mentioned not a single book.

Books were much more precious than swords and silver-gilt bowls and second-best beds in those days, and when a departing person owned one he gave it a high place in his will.

The will mentioned not a play, not a poem, not an unfinished literary work, not a scrap of manuscript of any kind.

Many poets have died poor. But this is the only one in history that has died this poor; the others all left literary remains behind. Also a book. Maybe two.

If Shakespeare had owned a dog—but we need not go into that . . .

This, again, from Mark Twain's essay **Is Shakespeare Dead**?

A few more "details" of interest have emerged since Samuel Clemens' time. That Shakespeare probably was apprenticed to a butcher, as a youth. Which could, of course, explain all his medical knowledge. That he might have fled to London after that episode of poaching deer. Hence his familiarity with archery. That he made a living in his early years in London holding horses outside the Globe, per Robert Greene's accusation that he was a "rude groome." Presumably composing *Hamlet* in his head, meanwhile. Hence his knowledge of chivalry.

We know now that Shakespeare, from the time of his arrival in London around 1587, was not doing "nothing," as Mark Twain supposed. But as we've seen, according to the only eyewitness, Robert Greene, what he was doing had nothing to do with the writing of plays. The official version is subject once again solely to supposition.

Biographer S. Schoenbaum makes this rather charming observation about that period: "Shakespeare's introduction to the Capital falls, frustratingly, in the void of the Lost Years, but legend has it filled with a pretty tale." Legend, not fact. In any case the tale so told is filled, alas, with "must haves," "reason to believes" "would haves," and "said to be's."

Nicholas Rowe, in his *Life of Shakespeare*, strove desperately to fill those blank spaces with hopeful surmise: "What particular habitude or Friendships he contacted with private Men I have not been able to learn. . ." Then he goes on to presume they "must have been" those with "A True taste for Merit" who "had generally a just Value and Esteem for him." Rowe didn't find any evidence of this. He just presumed it. He could come up with nothing further (and let us recall, this was Shakespeare's first biographer, the one closest to the source) except to conclude: "the character of the man is best seen in his writings." Possibly, but which man? And which writings?

In regards to source material, A.L. Rowse, another eminent biographer whose voluminous scholarly works are replete with his own fair share of "must have beens," citing "evidence from his plays" cautioned his readers thusly: "We must be on guard against the pedantry of source hunting!" Oh really? That's like telling a jury not to be blinded by mere facts. On the other hand, Rowse then confidently asserts: "Shakespeare is his own source." This must be so, because evidently the man had no others. And apparently neither did Rowse. The skeptics have not been silenced, for all the might of their opposition. Long-time U.S. research scholar Louis Ule found evidence that Shakespeare first went north to establish himself as a puppeteer in Lancashire, where a William Shakeshaft, an unemployed actor, is mentioned in a will dated August 3, 1581. Ule was a good enough detective to piece together the clues planted by Greene to fill in the so-called Lost Years. To recap: Shakespeare came to London around 1587, put on a veritable one-man-show as a puppeteer, worked as a groome and then started his horse valet service. He came to the attention of playwright Robert Greene when he began applying his business acumen towards becoming a moneylender and pawnbroker, especially of used costumes. He worked his way into the theater proper, first as a play prompter. Then, once establishing himself as a resident bit-part actor and play broker with the Admiral's (later Chamberlain's) Men, he was in the position to buy plays from the playwrights on behalf of the company.

One of those playwrights was Robert Greene, hence Greene's rage against the man for ripping him off, as he asserted in *Groatsworth of Wit*. Another such playwright was Christopher Marlowe. According to Greene, Shakespeare hired writers to work on plays for the company and possibly himself. We know he put his name on a lot of plays during that time. Even his staunchest defenders acknowledge he didn't write most of them. They even reject the so-called "bad Quartos" of *Henry VI* (1590). He did claim (or was given credit for) the three parts of the "good" *Henry VI*. Yet since then E.K. Chambers and most other scholars have conceded that Marlowe most likely wrote at least the second two parts.

It is reasonable to conclude from the evidence, therefore, that Shakespeare, in essentially a producer's chair, hired Christopher Marlowe to write that play. It is only after Christopher Marlowe is out of the picture, that the academic scholars can offer up any details at all as to Shakespeare's instantly successful literary career, always based on surmise.

Meanwhile, as far as the known facts go, all that can be said is that Shakespeare went on to become part owner of the Chamberlain's Men, the Blackfriars and later the Globe Theater companies. And that he made a lot of money.

Another thing we know that he did, which Twain neglected to mention, was to get himself involved in a lawsuit with a Huguenot family named Mountjoy, with whom he had lodged in Cripplegate, in London. The year was 1612, when he would have been at the zenith of his glory as the world's greatest poet and dramatist, about which there is no record. There is a record, however, of his active involvement with the Mountjoys over a matter that has nothing whatsoever to do with plays, playwriting, or even play brokering. The lawsuit was a family dispute, and Shakespeare, as a former lodger in their household (odd, considering his fame and fortune by then) was asked to give a deposition on the matter. This deposition provided one of the six existing signatures of the man. Never mind that each of those six signatures was written and spelled differently. The one thing they had in common was that they were scrawled. What the scholars have never acknowledged, and what is so significant about the Mountjoy deposition, is that Shakespeare could not remember one single detail regarding a matter some few years earlier. And yet at that same time he seemed able to remember enough actual names, places, and historical facts to write *Henry VIII,* and *King Lear* was yet to come. Could it be that our Bard was, well, a liar? If nothing else, that would be perfectly consistent with the character of the *Upstart Crow.*

Much of the debate over Shakespeare's authorship has boiled down to quibbling over commas and interpretations of dates, such as the William Ostler lawsuit in 1615 that refers to Shakespeare being already dead, depending on how one is to interpret a particular comma listing him with two other dead people. Boring! We don't need to go there. My detective's case is not dependent on dates or commas. His case is based on simple facts—and the lack thereof.

CLASS vs. BRASS

One final note regarding the Stratford "pedigree:"

Stratfordians have long comforted themselves with the certainty of their "heritage" by virtue of the fact that Shakespeare's father, John Shakespeare (the illiterate one) managed to acquire a coat of arms in 1596. Mind you, it was not William who got this, but his father, the elder Stratford butcher cum-farmer cum-glover. This brings to mind the claim by Edward de Vere's claimants, who base much of their own case on such evidence. It is patently bogus. Coats of arms then, as now, can be purchased by anyone vain enough to want one and jump through the necessary hoops to get it. Apparently John Shakespeare, coming into some money from uncertain sources (his son's business activities perhaps) thought it was time to join this Elizabethan equivalent of the country club.

One cannot buy nobility now, nor could one then. But a coat of arms required merely an application to the right person for a "patent," and, of course, a fee. Even so, the design had to be approved by the York Herald and the Garter King of the College of Arms, whose job is to say yea or nay. These two posts were held at the time of Shakespeare by Ralph Brooke and William Dethick, respectively. These two seemed to disagree over the qualifications of the good Shakespeare name even so, with Brook deriding Dethick for having granted the arms to "base persons," and Dethick firing back in defense of his actions. Brooke even referred scornfully to Shakespeare the son as a "common Player." Which is interesting, because by then the plays were all over the London stage, yet Brooke failed to mention Will's allegedly illustrious playwriting career at all. This is even more strange, since the author of the Plays, widely popular in the Queen's Court, would have been held in very high esteem indeed in courtly circles. Yet this heraldic dispute continued unabated until the Queen died, in 1603.

So much for public reverence of the great Shakespeare name, even at the height of son William's alleged career. Many writers go through life unrecognized or appreciated. But it isn't as though William Shakespeare of Stratford-upon-Avon never got his fifteen minutes. To the contrary he made a considerable mark in his time: as an agrarian businessman, moneylender and broker, who also worked in the theater business. All else written and said about him came long after the fact, and bears the unmistakable aroma, to anyone with a nose for it, of sheer Tonypandy.

Chapter Five

Shakespeare the Businessman

Here is where the pay dirt lies, for those seeking the truth about William Shakespeare. The only documentary evidence that exists of the man from Avon betrays about as ordinary, custom-bound, and shallow (if slightly unconventional) businessman, of the used-car lot variety. Nothing against businessmen, mind you, since that's what today's motion picture moguls still consider themselves (although they do have a tendency to believe they are artists, as well). Anyway, this leaves us to accept a probability along the lines of a plot from Monty Python, such as suggesting that it was Thomas Jefferson's neighborhood meat cutter who actually authored the U. S. Constitution and Bill of Rights. Shakespeare's recorded life, from beginning to end, is that of a businessman and nothing else. This is thoroughly documented by a variety of transactions: all of them involving one kind of business or another, none of them pertaining to arts, letters, theater, or drama, other than from a business perspective i.e. that of a studio executive or theater owner. Most of those transactions, which are dated throughout the span of his lifetime, have to do with the vocation into which he was born: agriculture. Others deal with moneylending, (usury) of which Robert Greene so bitterly accused him. Then of course there was his business interest in the Globe Theater itself. And before that his 1/16th share of the Blackfriars Theater, its predecessor. These financial shares in the company provided him with ample motivation to maximize his profit (as a good businessman does) by claiming authorship of the plays (as a film studio still does). The fact that he owned shares in the business of play-producing offers nothing in the way of proof as to authorship. But it offers a great deal in terms of insight as to Shakespeare's motivation as well as skill as a businessman.

Like most businessmen of his day as well as today, Shakespeare made no bones about trying to maximize profits by any means he could. One of the scant few documents in existence bearing Shakespeare's name reveals that the Privy Council of the time, in cracking down on the illegal and unethical practice of "hoarding" grain (thereby driving up the price) named Shakespeare of Stratford as a prime offender. He was charged with illegal possession of one hundred bushels or ten "quarters" of "corn" (wheat) during a time of severe shortages. Such shortages meant famine to some, in the face of which people began rightfully complaining to the authorities about the "maltsters," as they were called: "a nomber of wyked people in condiciones more lyke to wolves or cormorants than to natural men."

The people suffering these shortages at Shake-scene's hands went so far as to ask "If God send . . . Lord Essex down shortly, to see them hanged on gibbets at their own doors." This revelation led Charles Champlin of the Los Angeles Times to write:

"Did the man who hoarded grain at a time of famine also write (in *Hamlet* II, ii 317):

What a piece of work is man! How noble in reason! How infinite in faculty, in form and moving! How express and admirable in action! How like an angel in apprehension! How like a god!"

But then, perhaps "Shakespeare" was merely being cynical. Charles Champlin certainly was.

In furthering his case for Shakespeare's literacy, Irwin Matus tells us that the previously mentioned "only surviving" letter to Shakespeare, by his "good friend" Richard Quiney asking the moneylender for that loan, was evidence that Quiney would not have written to a man who could not read or write. But then Matus acknowledges that this letter was never mailed. Matus remarks, ironically, that the supporters of Shakespeare's chief rival, Edward de Vere (the 17th Earl of Oxford) would claim that this was due to Quiney's discovery, at the last moment, "that his good friend could not read after all." But no, he later reveals, the letter was not mailed because "it appears" Quiney had a meeting with the businessman and moneylender Shakespeare that very day in Stratford and didn't need to mail the letter. This supposition is based on another letter from Quiney written the same day to one Abraham Sturley, another local burgher, that "Shakespeare had helped promise to secure the loan."

Shakespeare was a very busy man indeed, it seems, since he was supposedly in London writing *Hamlet* at the time, and this was the year his name appeared in print on a Quarto for the first time (1597).

Aside from the rather naive assumptions as to the integrity of businessmen in general on which Matus' assertion is based, this claimed transaction was apparently a *fait accompli* the same day the first letter was written, and before the second went out. This in itself would elicit snickers from anyone who's ever dealt with either agents or producers in today's motion picture industry, and is simply a charming example of business practices since time immemorial. Here's how it works: Party "A," who wants something from Party "B," assures the latter that party "C" is already committed, thereby lending credence to the validity of party "A"'s enterprise, whatever it might be. In other words, it was, and is, common practice for loan seekers and dealmakers in general to assert that somebody else has promised (or bought into) whatever it is they're selling, and therefore you should too. In this way, by you saying yes, he or she can thereby quickly run back to the other party and inform him or her you're on board, and so they should be as well before it's too late, since you are such a brilliant and discriminating investor, etc. etc.!

All that any of this really accomplishes aside from further confirmation of Greene's charge of usury, is to underline what the biographers have consistently ignored: that Shakespeare was a businessman, and nothing more, busy in Stratford making deals when he was supposed to be in London writing plays, whether or not he could read. And while I don't wish to impugn the abilities or talents of businessmen in any way, it seems eminently clear to me that this Shakespeare was a factotum of one trade too many, none of which was a writer. As with the case of actors, businessmen and poets are simply not of the same mind set. Businessmen may have excellent literary skills, which they often apply to the composition of informative, frequently witty books and articles. About business. Businessmen are motivated by making money, not art. It is a rare thing indeed that a businessman turns out to be (or into) a great artist, closet or otherwise. Aside from Gaugin, we can think of Wallace Stevens and T. S. Elliot (both were bankers). But these were highly educated, scholarly and thoughtful men. Again there is no evidence Shakespeare the actor/entrepreneur was any of the above. And in general, business and art are simply too different from each other, as are the individuals who pursue those respective careers. Paul Gauguin had to quit his job and move to the South Seas before his art could develop and mature. Artists and writers take years to achieve a level of skill in the formation of lucid thoughts, expression of emotions and philosophies, the creative development of original imagery, and the accumulation of knowledge of history and human behavior. By the same token businessmen have to dedicate themselves to mastering a trade and making a profit, in order to succeed. In Elizabethan times, agrarian businesses such as those Shakespeare grew up in and returned to required one's full attention, or failure would be inevitable. One could not be a successful dilettante businessman/farmer then, or now, and succeed. Yet succeed in business Shakespeare certainly did, judging by the property he acquired before his "deseas."

Before you go off and accuse me of being a left wing anti-business ideologue, let me hasten to acknowledge that there is an important and vital interrelationship between art and business. Let's face it: business, at least in the U.S.A., provides most of the underwriting as well as end market for art. That there are philanthropic businessmen who are patrons and supporters of the arts there can be no doubt. In Europe most cultural institutions were supported by the nobility, and later the governments. But there would be few great museums or performance venues in the U.S.A. if it wasn't for private benefactors—wealthy businessmen with enough vision to understand that it took more than money to create a great civilization. Men like Carnegie, Rockefeller, Huntington, and most recently Getty and Soros, have given billions to support the arts.

Without such patronage, which in most countries was an artist's primary means of livelihood, the arts would wither and die. No great orchestra, for example, can survive just on ticket receipts. Someone has to come forward with substantial financial sponsorship in addition to whatever paltry government grants they can manage to garner to survive, and those individuals are invariably successful businessmen or women. Not that Shakespeare was ever any sort of philanthropist whatsoever, himself. Quite the opposite, if you look at the facts. The people like Shakespeare who owned and operated the theater companies in Elizabethan times, and those who run the film studios and television networks today, were and are business people. They may have artistic pretenses. Every film and television executive sees him or herself as a producer and script doctor, for example. They may have some training and background in the arts. But they are always businessmen (or women) in the end. The bottom line is profit, not art, and they will be the first to tell you so.

Of course, business people being business people, while many may be supportive of the arts—even patrons, even aficionados—many more are exploiters of the arts and the artists who create them. This is a time-honored practice, and Shakespeare fell into this category. The Globe Theater was a business, and their business was to acquire plays as cheaply as possible from playwrights, and make as much money as possible from their production. The same was true, and is true for the large corporate publishers today, not to mention Hollywood film producers. A business coup will always be at the expense of the artist or writer—so-and-so acquiring such-and-such for "a song." To the people who practice such, this is simply "good business."

Recently a TV commercial noted that Beethoven's 5th Symphony, "considered his greatest work" was bought for the equivalent of $20. The implication here is that the buyer was astute. A "good businessman."

No mention of how Beethoven might feel about it, in retrospect. Or have felt about it at the time. It was the best deal he could make in those days, no doubt. Nobody offered him more. He probably needed the money just to feed himself. And what is bad business for the artist is invariably good business for the play-broker, distributor, theater owner, or studio boss. To rip off the artist is what it's all about, today as in Elizabethan times. And the man who was in a position to do just that, possibly on behalf of Lord Strange's (amalgamated in 1589 with the Admiral's) Men and later on with the Chamberlain's/Hunsdon's Men, was William Shakespeare. Being an astute business entrepreneur in the manner of P.T. Barnum or Sam Goldwyn, in the end, may be where Shakespeare's true genius lay. Like Henry Ford, Sam Walton and others of our age who became zillionaires with little or no education, there is good evidence that Shakespeare accomplished something similar as a "Johannes factotum," playbroker and agribusiness entrepreneur. He had a way of getting people like Robert Greene to entrust him with their works, as well as their goods, and he squeezed them for all they were worth.

By 1594, with Greene dead and Marlowe gone less than a year, Shakespeare was a well-established power-broker and entrepreneur in the theater business, in a position to acquire his ownership share in the company: the next logical step for his suddenly skyrocketing career.

That was the year he became part-owner of the main production company of the time, the Chamberlain's Men, the company that would eventually perform in the Globe. Biographer A.L. Rowse confirmed that "he became a founding member of the Lord Chamberlain's Company in 1594, a sharer in its profits. They became the most successful company in London, and with these partners, his 'fellows' . . . he remained for the rest of his life. He then attained security and independence; freed from patronage." These things he did, but there is no evidence he did them as a playwright. For one thing, during the key years of 1589 to 1592, the principal playwright for the Admiral's Men was Christopher Marlowe, the most renowned playwright of the time. If Shakespeare was in fact also a part of this company as most scholars claim, he was never mentioned as a writer, and as a player only by hearsay.

All of the historical evidence as to Shakespeare's activities at that time is based on the usual surmise. Again, the only mention of his position in any capacity at all at that time was by Greene, and that was as the Johannes factotum discussed in Chapter 3. Edmund Malone wrote in his 1870 biography that Shakespeare's first position in the theater was that of "call boy." This too, is an important and overlooked signpost as to Shakespeare's true direction. "Call boy" is the natural predecessor to "prompter," and the prompter kept the playbooks. This would also be consistent with starting out as a groom, then a bit-player, who could do small roles in between other chores. In this capacity he was responsible for the plays from their entry into the theater to acceptance by the Master of Revels (the chief censor). It's an easy step from there to play-broker. But there's more. Alden Brooks noted that the Elizabethan prompter had charge not only of the plays, but also of props and apparel, including the buying and selling of costumes. Remember how Shake-scene had boasted to Greene of 200 pounds worth of "wearing apparrell" that he had pawned from the players, then out of work because of the plague? In addition to being further confirmation of Greene's claim that Shakespeare was a pawnbroker of costumes, this could well have been the same kind of "apparrell" he left to his sister "Jone" (sic) in his will. No books, but plenty of 'wearing apparrell.'

Getting back to Greene's wrathful charge of "Usurer," there is plenty of evidence of that. Shakespeare was clearly in the business of making loans. Aside from the Quiney loan letter there's another example from the London Public Record Office. In a lawsuit recorded in 1600, "William Shakspere" sued one John Clayton of Cheapside for seven pounds. This had been loaned in May, 1592, four months before Greene's invective. Shakespeare was himself sued for loans he never repaid, but he went after this one with a vengeance eight years after the fact, like a true moneylender. One would think a rich and successful world-class playwright would have more pressing pursuits. The evidence shows "Shakspere" the usurer-broker did not.

And so by 1592 Shakespeare was clearly in a position to buy plays, from Greene and from Marlowe, which led to all that outrage Greene unleashed in *Groatsworth of Wit* (Marlowe may have been in no position to complain, which I'll get to in Part II). That Shakespeare deliberately killed Robert Greene for denouncing him, as Ule implied, may be carrying it a bit far, and impossible to prove. Although any detective worth his donuts would feel compelled to at least take a look there. Still, lack of ethics as a businessman is one thing, to commit murder something else again. On the other hand, such practices were, and are, not unknown to ethically challenged loan sharks, which Shakespeare definitely was. Because there are more documents of fact pertaining to Shakespeare's loan sharking (two) than to his writing (none).

A second business coup for Shakespeare, starting five years later, would be the eventual publication of the playbooks for profit. Scholars have always agreed that the Quarto publications were pirated—that is, not authorized by the author, who was undoubtedly uncompensated. Yet Shakespeare himself never complained, even though he was money-conscious enough to have sued for seven pounds after eight years. In 1592 he was still operating as a usurer, yet it never occurred to his chroniclers that Shakespeare himself might be the pirate in question: putting his name on the plays and selling them for an additional profit. That would certainly explain his lack of outrage at their publication. Yet typically, the Stratford scholars have refused to accept or acknowledge the obvious, because, alas, it doesn't fit their preconceived construct of the myth upon which they have staked their many careers.

I can see Detective Grant piecing together the logical sequence, as groom became call boy, who became prompter and then play-broker. Shakespeare, never that interested in acting, gained control over the distribution of the playbooks and then the plays themselves. After a while, when he learned the ropes, he would realize he could make a nice additional profit by selling the playbooks to publishers, once the theatrical owners' interests in the properties had waned, and the plays were no longer being performed by the Players.

He would have been careful not to publish current plays. The theater owners, including Shakespeare himself, would have objected to that.

But if there was another way to make a shilling, he seemed to have a knack for finding it. As always, for him—ever the businessman—money was the bottom line.

Publishing in those days was a relatively new business—not yet seen as a path to fortune and fame. Shakespeare may have been the first to really see the profit potential in the publication of plays. Perhaps that, too, is where his true genius lay—again the businessman. But also a pirate. Therefore, a thief.

The hoarding-of-grain incident was not the only recorded lapse in Shakespeare's business ethics. A certificate of the London commissioners records that "William Shackspere" (another of his spellings), having made enough in the theater to return to his principal business of agriculture, left London for Stratford in 1597 without paying his taxes. It's in the record. William Shakespeare, tax evader. A lot of contemporary politicians would love this guy.

The new "Shakespeare's Globe Theater" in Southwark, London, located not far from the sites of the original Globe and Rose Theaters, has offered some interesting insights into Will Shake-scene's actual interest in the plays. Get this: Shakespeare, it seemed, had worked himself into a position in the company whereby he got paid three times for each performance: once as player (even though a bit player, he got a full share); once as co-owner (he owned ten percent, according to Shoenbaum and the Globe's own records); and a third time as playwright. Eat your heart out, Michael Ovitz! This latter payment is important, because it establishes a motive for the play-broker: he not only acquired plays for the company, but got a direct personal payoff from their acquisition. If he purchased them outright, which of course is possible (especially from playwrights such as Marlowe or Greene, who was desperate for a means to survive) he would have gotten a handsome return, aside from the credit (and credit is something no ethical person can simply purchase, although Hollywood's moguls certainly thought otherwise).

According to the new Shakespeare's Globe Theater, the cheapest ticket in Elizabethan times—for standing room among the 'groundlings'—was a penny. Again according to the Globe, an Elizabethan penny was essentially a day's wages for a worker. Or roughly 135 pounds in today's currency. There was room for five hundred groundlings, and another thousand seats in the covered boxes, ranging from sixpence to a shilling (twelve pennies) per seat. Plus extras, such as for cushions. It doesn't take a Rhodes Scholar to do the math. The shows were almost always sold out. This meant that the nightly take was something in the range of 5000 pence. Or, in today's numbers, about 25,000 pounds. So whatever the discount, Shakespeare's ten percent cut was considerable, and that was before the playwright's share, which was alone no small sum. It is small wonder he became a wealthy man owning so much "property." That he was a skilled and crafty businessman there is no doubt. But this has nothing to do with writing.

Chapter Six

Shakespeare and Hollywood

As I've pointed out, Shakespeare's believers, like most True Believers, have asked us, make that required us, to take his education, his accomplishments, his career on faith alone. Is this kind of magic without props even possible? Sure. In church. Or Hollywood.

Actor/players Matt Damon and Ben Affleck, for example, felt not the slightest twinge of remorse for suggesting that an unlettered bully from South Boston knew more about quantum physics than the entire M.I.T. faculty, in their screenplay *Good Will Hunting*. Never mind that his entire educational experience consisted of beating up tough guys in bar brawls. Once again, as the Shakespeareans love to say, "genius will find a way." Preferably with little or no effort. God forbid anyone should have to do some homework. The last hard-working hero who actually lifted a finger to accomplish his instant powers was Rocky, and even that was a pipe dream. In the film *Matrix* the hero downloads a computer program in twenty seconds flat, thereby providing him with all the super powers in the world. No exercise needed. Not even batteries. No wonder most modern parents can't get their kids to study French.

And so, at last, the true William Shakespeare emerges as the Elizabethan counterpart to a major Hollywood agent-turned-producer. He probably didn't know the word for "producer" yet, it was a whole new industry. But in many ways, based on Robert Greene's charges of plagiarism it would be no exaggeration to claim that Shakespeare, as the true predecessor to men such as Samuel Goldwyn and Louis B. Mayer, was, indeed, The Man Who Invented Hollywood. Of course, some questions will remain. Such as how, exactly, did Shakespeare and his supporters get away with it? How was it that Will Shake-scene, country bumpkin turned entrepreneur, could pull off what in retrospect has to be the most spectacularly successful art theft in history? Of not only a wealth of "property," but an entire literary career and legacy?

Once again, one need look no further than our present day equivalent to the popular entertainment medium that was the Elizabethan theater—Hollywood—to find the answers. In Hollywood one will find a distinct and intriguing parallel between the business practices of Shakespeare and company, and those of many latter day agents, producers and studio owners. A good detective, had he looked, could have construed long ago by close examination of the dubious package of properties "Written by W.S." or "William Shakespeare," that the whole thing was a product. A brand name like "Betty Crocker" (who didn't actually exist). A good comparison to this would be the Samuel Goldwyn Studios. Samuel Goldwyn's own career paralleled that of Shakespeare in remarkable ways. Before getting into the film business, Goldwyn sold gloves for a living. (His most famous quote, incidentally, was "include me out"). Another example of a theatrical company with a name attached to a product line is, of course, the Walt Disney Company. Except that once upon a time at least, Walt Disney personally created animated cartoons. Himself. It was only later when he became an institution that he stamped his name on everything the company produced, while the real artists and writers remained anonymous (and effectively remain so today). Virtually all of the factual evidence about the theatrical career of Will Shakespeare boils down to this: he was listed as a player with the Chamberlain's Men, and an owner/partner in the company. Period. As an actor, Rowe wrote that he could not find any record of his playing any important roles, and that "the top of his performance was the ghost in . . . *Hamlet*."

In the 1950's, the best and brightest of Hollywood's writers, members of the Screen Writer's Guild as it then called itself, were accused of being communists or communist sympathizers by the House Un-American Activities Committee, chaired by U. S. congressman Parnell Thomas. The Star Chamber of its time, the committee itself was unconstitutional, since the First Amendment to the Bill of Rights of the Constitution of the United States precludes legislation governing one's thoughts or beliefs. The "Hollywood Ten," as they became known (seven of whom were screenwriters) were stripped of all credits, all stature, and their very livelihoods during this political witch-hunt. This practice, known as "blacklisting," lasted fifteen years and was to damage or destroy the careers of hundreds of people before it was all over. In Elizabethan times the Star Chamber was also illegal because it operated out of sight of Parliament. Yet this is exactly how Christopher Marlowe was condemned in 1593. As in the case of Marlowe's colleague Thomas Kyd in the hands of the Elizabethan Privy Council, the only way to avoid imprisonment if subpoenaed by such an illegal committee was to "cooperate." And the way to "cooperate" with HUAC in Washington was the same way that Marlowe's compatriot Thomas Kyd was forced to cooperate with the Elizabethan Privy Council in London—name names or you're dead meat. Kyd named Marlowe. Actor Ronald Reagan and director Elia Kazan named names in Hollywood. The famous Hollywood Ten who were named refused to cooperate, and went to jail. All of them. They were: Producer Adrian Scott, directors Edward Dmytryk and Herbert Biberman, and writers John Howard Lawson, Ring Lardner, Jr., Samuel Ornitz, Alvah Bessie, Lester Cole, Albert Maltz and Dalton Trumbo, who I met myself years later. Some of those blacklisted writers still managed to find work, usually for substandard wages because they had lost the protection of their Guild. But they were the best writers in the business, and the producers needed them. So they worked under *nom de plumes*, or not at all. This practice continued until the early 1960's, when producer Otto Preminger decided enough was enough, and openly hired Dalton Trumbo to write the screenplay for *Exodus*. Many of the "Ten" were dead by then, and it wasn't until 1985 that, in a brief display of calculated remorse, the motion picture industry began restoring credits to those who'd actually earned them. The widows of Carl Foreman and Michael Wilson (blackballed but not jailed) received the Oscars their husbands should have gotten in 1957 for *The Bridge on the River Kwai*. It wasn't until 1992 that Dalton Trumbo was restored his credits for *Roman Holiday, The Brave One* and *Gun Crazy*. Similarly Albert Maltz (*Broken Arrow*) and Ned Young (*The Defiant Ones*) received their long overdue credits. And it wasn't until 1995 that Michael Wilson was finally recognized as co-author with Robert Bolt for *Lawrence of Arabia*.

As an interesting sidebar to all of this, Michael Wilson also wrote another award-winning screenplay, *The Friendly Persuasion*, a copy of which Ronald Reagan gave to Mikhail Gorbachev at their famous Helsinki meeting. Typically, Reagan, who as President of the Screen Actor's Guild was a leading prosecution witness for HUAC in the 1950s, never even knew the true writer's name or his own role in Wilson's demise. Nor has Reagan ever admitted that blacklisting even took place. But then he didn't know about Iran-Contra, either.

Because of this paranoia-induced miscarriage of justice, many of the names that appeared on the best films of that era were a complete fiction—names either made up, or belonging to another—either by complicity or convenience. All in all, according to the Writer's Guild of America, the writing credits for 24 films were taken from their writers, and not restored until nearly fifty years after the blacklisting of writers began.

What is so fascinating is how exactly history repeated itself, or more accurately predicted itself, in the case of Christopher Marlowe. He was being hunted to the ground by the HUAC of his time, the Star Chamber (no need to comment on the most recent manifestation, the Starr Chamber that hounded President Clinton for his peccadilloes) who were embroiled in a witch-hunting frenzy of their own. Accusations had been made and inquiries had been ordered by Archbishop of Canterbury John Whitgift against the free thinkers of Elizabethan times—"Raleigh's Circle" or "Raleigh's School of Night" as they were known, for their leader Sir Walter Raleigh (himself later executed). This group consisted of the pre-eminent artists, scholars, scientists and literati not just of England but all of Europe, including, at times, Galileo, Spenser, Giordano Bruno and Thomas Harriot. Among them were Christopher Marlowe and possibly his patron Sir Thomas Walsingham (no sign of Shakespeare). Questioning ecclesiastical or political orthodoxy was, of course, considered heresy. And "Heresy" was the Communism of the Middle Ages.

"DIRECTED BY ALAN SMITHEE"

The Director's Guild of America, the eminent and highly prestigious organization that represents motion picture and television film directors in all negotiations with the producers and management of film studios and television networks, has a longstanding practice involving the use of pseudonyms (Mark Twain was, of course, himself a pseudonym). I wouldn't call it policy as it is not legally defined, but it comes into play when directors are unable or unwilling to assume or accept credit for the directing of a motion picture set for release. When this situation occurs, by tacit agreement among the members the credit will read as follows: Directed by Alan Smithee. That being, of course, a generic pseudonym. While this is usually done only when the film is so dismally bad the director wants to deny creative responsibility, sometimes it is called for due to reasons other than "creative differences." Sometimes the director cannot be identified for political or other reasons.

This practice is well known in the motion picture industry, but virtually unknown to the general public. So let us hypothesize for a moment. Suppose, after all these years, someone whose actual name was Alan Smithee stepped forward and proclaimed himself to be the "real Alan Smithee" with a birth certificate to prove it. This person could conceivably thereby claim all credit for all those 'Alan Smithee' films (good or otherwise) and along with that credit, at least in theory, all due financial participation, residuals, and so forth. In other words, even in today's sophisticated, highly visible business-oriented film industry with detailed contracts between producers, networks, and the professional guilds of Directors, Writers and Screen Actors in particular, someone could claim or assume credits they didn't earn.

This, to quote Chambers, Rowse, Robertson and the others, "may well have been" what happened in the case of "William Shakespeare," when no such Guilds or protections existed. This practice of taking (or giving) an unearned credit is far more endemic than one might suspect, even today. Especially when it comes to credits awarded to writers for film and television screenplays. Even when the writers have signed contracts, registered copies, established all sorts of proof that they were the original creators of a script or screenplay, final arbitration of credits nowadays, in the USA at least, must still be decided by a panel designated by the Writers Guild of America (of which I am a member). This came about due to practices in the early days of the industry in which producers were notorious for assigning credits to wives, concubines, bookies, agents, and players-to-be-named-later. And it still happens today because it is common practice now, in this industry, for studios or producers to hire subsequent writers to rewrite a screenplay. The original script may be perfect. This doesn't matter in the least.

Often, rewriting is done simply to remove the original writer from any ownership, involvement, or participation in the creative decisions or final product. This involves employment of several writers for that purpose alone, and is common practice even when the original writer may have conceived the story, characters, plot and basic premise from scratch, or even from his or her own life, or book. Because of this practice the Writer's Guild of America finally began to intercede, demanding final say in credit arbitration as part of their hard-won Basic Agreement with the Motion Picture and Television Producers Association of America—the umbrella organization that governs all film and television contracts. The way it works is a Guild-appointed committee of writers must anonymously decide who should get credit even when it should be painfully obvious from the get-go. This is done automatically when there is more than one writer involved, which is almost invariably the case. Often a director will rewrite a script merely to force this issue, sometimes managing by doing so to claim credit for the entire film. At the very least, he or she will do so in hopes of attaining at least a shared credit of someone else's work. Plus, a recent innovation, designed as a final insult to writers, is the so-called "possessory credit," which consists of the director's name above the title, as in "An Alan Smithee Film."

For an actor to take credit for a writer's work is certainly nothing new, either. It is a time-honored practice, as common in Hollywood today as it was in Elizabethan times. Except in Elizabethan times there were no copyrights, no writers or authors' guilds, and in general no scruples about "borrowing" or stealing from the works of others. They called it "witching up," in those days. Few of the brokers and publishers who registered plays with the Company of Stationers even bothered to attach a name to them. In light of this, it is especially notable that the famed invective by Robert Greene in 1592 was directed against one "player" in particular: the only one in the business who was also prompter, agent, broker, usurer, groom, and factotum.

In all fairness to thespians, it must be acknowledged that the plays, despite what the 19th Century scholars (particularly Alexander Pope) professed, were written to be performed, not read. As William Hazlett wrote in 1841, the plays were "expressions of passions, not descriptions of them. His characters are real beings of flesh and blood; they speak like men, not like authors" (God forbid anyone should speak like an author!), performed by actors, who brought all those wonderful characters to life. The problems in this relationship arose, always, when actors chose or were allowed to interpret or rewrite (or even delete) the words of the playwright to suit their own purposes. Sometimes this form of collaboration prospered. But usually when changes occurred, as with the early Quartos, they were for the worse and at the expense of the author and the integrity of the play itself. It was even worse if the author was not present or available to defend his words. Writers are still not allowed on the set at most film productions. And in the theater, especially the Elizabethan theater that had few sets or effects (with the notable exception of Marlowe's plays) and minimum props, the words were everything.

The Chamberlain's Men, which acquired the plays, were every bit as corporate and profit-based as a present-day movie studio. Here again, the film industry analogy serves well. God help any aspiring screenwriter who gives a script to a Hollywood actor. Let alone a producer or studio executive, without an accredited agent representative or lawyer's intervention. The streets of Los Angeles have long echoed with the lamentations of writers who were ill-served by those they entrusted with their works. And so it was that William Shakespeare, as an acting partner in a theatrical company (the Chamberlain/King's Men) and later part-owner of the Globe Theater, had access, and would have frequently acquired ownership—often for a few shillings—of the works of others. How easy it would have been, and was, for an unscrupulous businessman/theater owner (the equivalent of a producer), like the unscrupulous grain merchant Shakespeare also was, to take advantage of the situation. Irwin Matus observed that no one would know better how to stage a play than an actor, as further evidence supporting Shakespeare as author, while overlooking the obvious: that staging is not the equivalent of writing. Kit Marlowe, on the other hand, was both a playwright and an amateur actor. It was compulsory in those days for students at Cambridge to participate in the theater, at risk of expulsion.

Kit Marlowe would understand the conflicts involved: how the interaction of thespians might be conducive to play composition—rehearsing, experimenting with lines, sharing of knowledge of languages and foreign places and so forth, while at the same time being a constant threat to the integrity of the original artist's (author's) vision. And vision is the key word here. Nothing in Shakespeare's life (or will) demonstrated any vision at all. Au contraire Christopher Marlowe, whose literary and theatrical vision, even in his early plays (those that actually bear his name) was stunning. But more on Marlowe later.

Chapter Seven

Where there's a Will

It is a sad reality of life that, unlike in the movies, the good guy does not always win. Ask any real-life police detective. Or voter. Many are the crooks, impostors, politicians, murderers and usurpers who have died wealthy, happy, and unpunished (at least in this world.) Will Shakspur/Shakespeare may eventually prove to be one of the best examples. And yet how easily, once again, a good detective could have found him out long, long ago. Perhaps the best clue of all in the case against Shakespeare as poet and playwright was the man's own will.

His memory was as lacking as his art by 1612, when he gave that Mountjoy deposition, in which he couldn't remember a thing. But it was apparently much improved by 1616, when he wrote his will: the only handwritten document in existence that bears his signature(s).

Josephine Tey's police detective Grant would surely find William Shakespeare's Last Will and Testament fascinating. He would insist on seeing a copy with the original text, not the one certain Stratfordians have taken upon themselves to grammatically renovate. It is readily available in *The Riverside Shakespeare*, among other sources.

The will, discovered in 1747 by the cleric Joseph Greene (the one who re-invented the famous bust of the Bard now on display in Stratford) is the only undisputed documentary evidence of anything ever "written" by Shakespeare, aside from that intellectually challenged stone epitaph.

As Mark Twain pointed out, the will included not a single book, letter, manuscript, reference or allusion in any way to a life as a literary man. This extraordinary point of fact once again the Stratford gang has blithely and successfully dismissed as meaningless, while at the same time touting the will's significance as further documentary evidence of the man's stature in Stratfordian affairs. It's as though this will somehow replaces the missing evidence of literacy. E. K. Chambers suggests that the lack of mention of books is only because they were "probably" included in the "household goods." Along with the cutlery, perhaps. The Stratfordians, with their circular logic, insist on having it both ways as usual. They claim on the one hand that books are rare and valuable treasures and it's therefore unreasonable to assume that just everybody would have some, even if one does happen to be the world's greatest writer and therefore presumably a reasonably literate man. And then they circle back to claim that even if one did happen to have some of these rare treasures, they'd just be part and parcel of the household goods, along with the pots and pans and dirty linens, in no way as valuable as, say, one's "second best bed." One can only concede that since Shakespeare's wife and daughters couldn't read in any case, perhaps there would be little point in leaving them books. Yet the Bard's great counterpart on the stage, Edward Alleyn (also self-educated) left a substantial library in his will, along with papers and manuscripts, among them an anonymous Thomas More play (more on this later). And he never claimed to be an author.

The will itself is a profoundly damning document, which is why so many Stratfordians must either correct or ignore the hundreds of spelling and grammatical errors throughout the text, not to mention the punctuation, of which the will had none. This kind of alteration, in legal terms, is known as tampering with the evidence. Once so confronted, others rush to claim that it was actually penned by a scrivener on behalf of an attorney, and the rampant illiteracy of the document is to be blamed on its "real" writer or writers. But their own cleverness is their undoing here. E.K. Chambers concludes that the text was "probably" in the hand of a clerk employed by Francis Collins, a solicitor of Warwick who "probably" drafted the will. Collins was the will's executor so this is a fair assumption. But Chambers also acknowledges that Shakespeare had to have composed it. Since other Stratfordians have proposed that Shakespeare's marvelous command of legal terminology and nuance results from his having "no doubt" "interned" in his youth with a local Stratford lawyer, one can only assume that it wasn't the likes of Mr. Collins. Chambers and others note that he made numerous corrections. None of them, unfortunately, addressed the questions of spelling and grammar. William Shakespeare willingly signed this document three times (with a variety of spellings). Again, this remains his only positively identified written work, containing half of his known signatures, each one scrawled and spelled differently.

Chambers dismisses the problems of spelling and punctuation as consistent with the work of lawyer Collins, whose draftsman may have even signed it for the ailing Shakespeare, thereby absolving Shakespeare of any responsibility whatsoever for its lack of form or content. However, paleographer Charles Hamilton, in his book *In Search of Shakespeare* is convinced, through handwriting analysis, that Shakespeare composed the will in his own hand: signatures and all.

Following are some examples of the text of the will:

From Sheet one:

I Willem Shackspeare . . . in perfect health and memorie.. (Quite a recovery from his Mountjoy deposition four years earlier, in which he couldn't remember a thing). He says "after my deceas" eight times. He says "that is to say" twice on the first sheet followed by such grammatically challenged phrases of homespun legalese as these: ". . . so long time as . . ." "that she now hat of in or to . . ." "shall like of to . . ." ". . . three Yeares next ensueing the daie of the date . . ." ". . . my will ys that she shall have the consideracion to bee paied to her children if she have

Anie & if not to her executours or assignes she lyving the said term after my deceas . . ." "All my wearing Apparrell to be paied & deliuered w(ith)in one yeare after my deceas . . ." (This last line harkens back to Robert Greene's charge that he was a pawnbroker of player's apparel, since he obviously considers it a form of currency, if not chattel.) He then signs the first sheet: William Shakspere.

From Sheet two:

"Ffyve poundes A peece." "I give (a number of people including his actor colleagues Hemminge, Condell & Burbage) a Peece to buy him rings . . ." then: ". . . for better enabling of her to performe this my will . . ." (his daughter, Susanna Hall, apparently also an actor).

Then follows the longest run-on sentence in history, which, while not technically in error, grammatically-speaking, does seem somewhat devoid of the usual Shakespearean flair. This goes on for several hundred words including several more "Deceas"es, now capitalized, then yet another Shakespearism is revealed: "To Have and to Hold," this time referring to real estate).

Shakespeare's defenders may rightly point out that many or most wills contain lots of boring language. But language was supposed to be the great legacy, even currency of this man. Could he not have been more artful in his final statement? (Well, judging by the epitaph, I guess not.) The will proceeds: "to the heires Males of the bodie of the saied third sonne lawfullie yssuing And for defalt of such issue the same soe to be (or not to be!) & Remaine . . . (signed:) Willm Shakspere. (And then the third sheet, where this wealthy man gives his "second best bed" to his wife and finally:) "By me William Shakspeare."

"By me?" Not, "I do hereby swear as to the veracity of my signature," or "In good faith with God and these my friends as my witnesses," or "I do hereby attest to the correctness and accuracy of these the terms of my will." Only, "by me." Maybe he was tired, after that hundred-word run-on list of barns. One can just see him signing *Othello* that way, then thumping his chest with his last ounce of vainglorious energy: "I wrote that! Yessir, that there showplay was 'by me!'" Of course, the Stratfordians insist the will wasn't "by me" at all, but by a grammatically challenged lawyer named Francis Collins. And he had an education!

In any case, Shakespeare ends this embarrassment with the fourth different spelling of his own name in one document. But then this shouldn't surprise us, as he did the same on the Quartos, each one printed with a different version of the name. It's almost as though he never quite got a handle on his own name, and needed much more practice with his writing than a mere 36 plays (not including the bad ones) and a hundred plus sonnets would allow.

Even the truest Believer must surely lament the lack of some last fleeting visionary thought, some final word of wisdom, of wit, of art, something for his by-then myriad dedicatees, using at least a few of those artful contents of his 16,000 word vocabulary. But no. It's all barns, and bodies, beds and bumpkinisms. Alas, poor Shakespeare, we knew him not at all.

In the end, Mark Twain said it best: this was a country businessman's will, not an author's. The signatures on this will are the only academically approved, officially accepted fully confirmed samples in existence, aside from the signatures on the Mountjoy deposition and the Blackfriars gatehouse documents, of "The Bard's" handwriting. Even this fact, however—so important to Stratfordians to counter charges that their man couldn't write at all—is in hot dispute. Sir George Greenwood claimed that, as evidenced by the "X" with which he signed his wedding certificate, Shakespeare was so completely illiterate he needed a clerk to inscribe even his earlier signatures. In this regard, Sir Edwin Durning-Lawrence concluded that all six signatures were facsimiles written by clerks, proving that Shakespeare could not write at all. This view is bolstered by Durning-Lawrence's finding that the Mountjoy signature was a perfect match to the handwriting of a known law clerk of the times. Charles Hamilton sharply refutes this, demonstrating through handwriting comparisons that there are sufficient similarities in the signatures, spelling differences notwithstanding, to conclude them to be the man from Stratford's, further strengthening his claim that they match the handwriting in the will itself. Hamilton further professes to have found another previously unrecognized signature in the "Shakespeare-Replingham Agreement." This is a 1613 legal contract between Shakespeare and a neighbor regarding a tithe for the grazing of sheep. Hamilton exultingly proclaims that Shakespeare wrote the whole thing! Yet another addition to the Bard's biographical and literary legacy. Unfortunately, like all the other existing documents chronicling the man's life, it has nothing to do with plays, poems, or prose.

Paleographer Charles Hamilton does offer up one optimistic note for the Stratford faithful, however: he believes that portions of the three sheets of the anonymously written play *Sir Thomas More* are, in fact in Shakespeare's hand. Several other handwriting experts led by Professor Samuel A. Tannenbaum have previously made this claim, based on the signatures, that Shakespeare was the author. This is intended to prove his legitimacy not only as one who can write wills and sheep deals, but plays as well. Stratfordians themselves have embraced this Thomas More revelation with little enthusiasm. And those who have, should not have done so. The play is an embarrassment, especially if written, as Tannenbaum suggests, in 1593, the year of *Venus and Adonis*. Aside from its wearisome pedestrian content, it is as grammatically wanting, as lacking in art as, well, Shakespeare's will. If anything, the play can be added to the list of embarrassments Stratfordians have been forced to explain away.

Marlowe biographer Calvin Hoffman wondered why Shakespeare's early chroniclers didn't bother to interview the Bard's own family. Nicholas Rowe's *Life* would not be published until nearly a hundred years after Shakespeare's death (1709). Surely the sources of Rowe's material—the recounts and recollections of Shakespeare's "peers" such as Sir William Davenant, could and should have included an interview or two with at least one of Shakespeare's daughters.

Susanna Hall lived at Stratford until 1649, and his other daughter Judith Quiney lived there until 1662. Then there was his granddaughter Elizabeth Hall Nash-Bernard, who lived until 1670. One can only speculate that while any sensible inquirer after the world's greatest playwright and poet would have troubled to talk to those who knew him best, perhaps they found such interviews wanting.

Evidence of this can be found in Chambers' *Problems*. Sir William Oldyce reported that Shakespeare's younger brother (presumably Edmund) lived in London for many years after the alleged poet's death, was widely sought out by players and others seeking information about the Bard, but "he could give them but little light into their inquiries, and all that could be recollected from him of his brother Will . . . was having once seen him act a part in 'one of his own comedies.'" The term "his" would seem important, implying a claim of ownership. But this claim of ownership is a claim every film director, leading player or producer routinely makes in today's motion picture business, as I've already pointed out. That Stratfordian scholars have routinely used this brother's sparse anecdotal tale as evidence Shakespeare was a writer is not surprising. But ownership can simply mean you bought something. Or successfully stole it (finders keepers, etc.). This story is apocryphal, in any case, since all three of Shakespeare's younger brothers died before he did, the last (Richard) in 1613. Edmund, the one described as "A Player," died in 1607. So if Oldyce was right about the interview taking place and simply got the years wrong, Edmund knew nothing of his brother's writing activities even at the peak of Will's alleged career.

It is easy to understand how the younger brother might enjoy the vicarious fame that came of ownership, without caring to divulge that his elder sibling was not actually, to his knowledge, any sort of writer whatsoever. On the other hand, as Edmund, too, was apparently an ignorant man, he may have merely, as Oldyce suggests, been simple-minded. This is a role that Will Shakespeare would have related to, having played it more than once himself on the stage. In any case Shakespeare died as he lived, producing and leaving nothing of tangible substance except money and property. More to the point, he died fat and happy, perhaps content in the knowledge that he had gotten clean away with the greatest art theft of all time.

Chapter Eight

The Noble Cause

As Mark Twain observed, by the end of the 19th Century the Authorship of the Shakespeare Canon was in hot dispute. So who was the true author, who either allowed, or was forced to accept Shakespeare's usurping of his life's works? Today's current front-runner for this title is an obscure 16th century gadabout named Edward de Vere, the 17th Earl of Oxford. Thanks to the relentless campaigning of the de Vere heirs, bolstered by the writings of B. M. Ward and Charlton Ogburn, the so-called Oxfordians (no connection to the famed university) have forged their way to the lead in this quest for the throne of literary kingship and the crown of world's greatest poet and playwright.

What Edward de Vere has going for him, other than that he wrote a few passing-fair poems, is snob appeal. That plus the intense lobbying efforts of these tireless champions. There is no evidence de Vere was ever anything more than a spoiled dilettante with too much idle time on his hands. At a recent lecture in Los Angeles one of the world's leading de Vere scholars (who has requested anonymity) admitted that after twenty-five years of studying de Vere's poetry, along with other lesser-known Elizabethans, he could see no similarity between de Vere's style in poetry and that attributed to Shakespeare.

He said, "Believe me, if I thought there was any chance he might have had anything to do with it, I would be thrilled; I would be in a great position; but I have to tell you, in my opinion de Vere has no connection to Shakespeare's works."

Charleton "shakes a spear" Ogburn seems to have overlooked this discrepancy. Instead, he hypothesizes that it was "well known" the 17th

Earl was already using the pen name "Shake-spear" by then, 14 years before the first Work of any kind was published (*Venus and Adonis*). Again, much is made of the necessity for a nobleman to disguise his literary aspirations, which were in fact discouraged in those times. But, as Shakespeare scholar Irwin Matus points out in his book *Shakespeare, in Fact*, if de Vere's pen name was so "well known," and his intentions were to conceal his identity, what was the point of using it?

Also, what evidence is there to confirm this allegedly widely held knowledge? Harvey's quote, plus the fact that one of the Earl's lesser titles—that of Viscount of Bulbeck—had a badge depicting a lion shaking a broken spear—is the sum total of his evidence. The rest is speculation. And this great "revelation" proves even less remarkable than it sounds, considering that badges of lions shaking spears were about as unremarkable in those days as flags with colorful stripes are today. Still, if one insisted on pursuing that argument—that the 17th Earl of Oxford would choose as the symbol of his life's work the emblem of an obscure Viscount, the cuteness of such a pointless ploy seems as meaningful as suggesting that the U. S. Democratic Party adopted the donkey as their symbol because President Andrew Jackson's nephew used to own one.

"Shake-spear" in Harvey's context referred to the posturing of war. In Robert Greene's *A Groatsworth of Wit*, which identifies William Shakespeare as "Shake-scene," the reference was pompous theatrics. In neither case can it be connected to literary endeavor. And yet if Edward de Vere and the Stratford loyalists have anything at all in common, it is that this business of spear-shaking is all the evidence they really have connecting their respective heroes to the Works. That, and the Shakespeare "Title page" conundrum.

In all fairness, no one questions that the Earl of Oxford was a patron of the arts who "actively encouraged" the literary scene in the 1570's. He was "instrumental in the publication of *Cardanus's Comfort* (1573) and very probably did play an active role in the poetry anthology, *A Hundred Sundrie Flowres* (also 1573). The fortuitous circumstances of having John Lyly in his service at a time when entertainments at court could enhance his standing with the queen resulted in two of the greatest court comedies in her reign": *Sapho and Phao* and *Campaspe* (both 1584). But these were either written entirely by his company (Oxford's Men)'s resident playwright John Lyly, or by Lyly in collaboration with de Vere. While he may have collaborated with Lyly, there is no evidence of de Vere ever having written a play himself. And as for the argument that de Vere may have ceded credit for his own works to Lyly, it is far more probable that this vainglorious man would have tried to take credit for himself—if not then, at least later. Likewise regarding the Shakespeare Canon.

All that is known about de Vere suggests a childish ego that could not have withstood anonymity for long. Especially for works that would become so highly regarded during his own lifetime. As with Shakespeare himself, there are no autographed manuscripts or printed texts linking de Vere to the Works, or any works other than sixteen poems. Stratfordians have acknowledged that Shakespeare must have had collaborators—in particular Christopher Marlowe's Cambridge protege John Fletcher on *Henry VIII* and Marlowe himself on *Henry VI Parts II* and *III*, among others. But Fletcher's hand on *Henry VIII* proves highly inconvenient for the de Vereians, because Fletcher didn't even begin writing until 1608—five years after de Vere's death.

Because Edward de Vere did write some poems, his partisans have also tried to use those poems to bolster their case for him citing similarities in the context and meaning of certain of his phrases to Shakespeare's. Unfortunately, as it turns out, the poems in question weren't even written by de Vere, but by Robert Greene, Thomas Campion and Fulke Greville. So de Vere's claims to Shakespeare's titles are not only suspect. They are phony. Furthermore, de Vere's partisans attempted, beginning with Alexander Grosart's edition of his poetry in 1872, to grossly inflate the number of poems he wrote, even crediting him with songs from Lyly's plays, and eleven works "arbitrarily selected" from *England's Helicon*.

De Vere was patron to a company of boy players of the 1580's, and a few anonymous plays of little note were registered and performed by "Oxford's Men" in 1600-01. De Vereians have tried to bolster the importance of this small-time theatrical troupe that played at such notable arts houses as the Boar's Head Inn (a pub) by suggesting that de Vere was the real "Lord Chamberlain" of the Chamberlain's/King's Men, which was, of course, Shakespeare's company. The problem here is that the real Lord Chamberlain of the time and a known patron of that company was Henry, Lord Hunsden, the Lord Chamberlain to the court of the Queen.

Again, to provide some sort of foundation for their highly speculative case for de Vere, de Vereians have attempted to demonstrate that many of Shakespeare's plays were really about him and his family. For example, J. Thomas Looney wrote a synopsis of *All's Well that Ends Well* that "perfectly matches" de Vere's personal life story. Except that it doesn't. What it does perfectly match is the 9th Story, Day Three of Boccaccio's *Decameron*. So far the de Vereians have not ventured to claim that he wrote that, also. Next, Ogburn has made a poignantly emotional claim that only de Vere could have written *Hamlet*, based on his certainty that the characterization of Polonius had to have been a lampoon of Lord Burghley, who helped raise the ungrateful de Vere. (Burghley, incidentally, was also mentor to Christopher Marlowe).

Ogburn doesn't explain why de Vere would lampoon his own patron and mentor so harshly. Burghley was by all accounts a wise and well-thought-of man in the Queen's court, unlike de Vere himself.

Lord Burghley bent over backwards for his young charge time and again, and was little rewarded for his efforts. Shakespeare scholar S. Schoenbaum has observed the same regarding Marlowe, that he had ill cause to lampoon Burghley. But only the de Vereians have claimed the Burghley connection. Kit Marlowe was forced to face indictment by Burghley's Privy Council in the end, and besides, he had other role models to choose from. There is one parallel to Hamlet's life in de Vere's—he did marry Burghley's daughter, and treated her miserably. But unlike Hamlet at the death of Ophelia, de Vere didn't even bother to show up for his wife's funeral when she died.

De Vere himself was a consummate ne'er-do-well, who never held a job other than the ceremonial post of "Lord High Chamberlain," which had nothing to do with the real Chamberlain's job, the important position held by Lord Hundsen. Through constant profligate behavior, mostly at the expense of his beleaguered mentor Lord Burghley, de Vere eventually fell into permanent disfavor with the Queen. Fed up with his philandering with her serving girls (impregnating at least one) and incurring bad debts in Burghley's name, Queen Elizabeth banished him from court for good around 1590.

Even this disgrace the de Vereians have tried to turn to their favor, suggesting that this was the time de Vere did his writing, apparently forgetting that he was already "well known" as "Shake-spear" in 1587. Except what he mostly did, for the rest of his life, was to scheme for money, concocting plots in his efforts to monopolize various commodities such as wool, fruits and tin. In this sense he had a lot in common with Shakespeare, the Stratford businessman, except that Shakespeare was a lot more successful.

Edward de Vere was the Elizabethan equivalent of a spoiled prodigal who couldn't manage his own affairs, let alone write about them. But yet again, de Vere's supporters come to his rescue. When the Queen took pity on him (at the request of Lord Burghley) and allotted him a stipend of a thousand pounds a year for his living expenses (a truly princely sum) Ogburn and Ward suggest that this was actually payment for writing all those great plays. Except if poetry and playwriting were off limits for a nobleman (therefore requiring use of a pen name) it didn't seem to bother Sir Philip Sidney any. He was one of the most highly regarded men (and poets) in the realm, noble or otherwise. And if writing was such a declasse pasttime, de Vere could hardly claim said authorship in order to take such payment, nor did he.

And unless he'd "outed" his secret literary life, how (and why) would the Queen know to reward him for said Works?

Matus also points out that the Queen would not have held the man who was "Shakespeare" in such poor regard, because his Works, played frequently in Court continually pleased and delighted her, with the singular exception of the ill-timed performance of *Richard II*, in 1601 (see Part II Chapter 9). In fact, biographer Nicholas Rowe noted that "Queen Elizabeth had several of his Plays acted before her and without doubt gave (the author) many gracious Marks of her favor."

So again, knowing this, de Vere would have had every reason to own up to his little nom de plume and claim those "Marks of favor" for himself. If anything, ownership of such extraordinary accomplishment could only have improved his low standing with her Majesty.

De Vereians have numerous other hurdles to overcome in making their claim, such as the timing of the plays' publication. De Vere died in 1604, which is very inconvenient, and which date has not been refuted. Since this date obviously requires that all of the Works be written before that time in order to allege authorship by de Vere, this has required the Earl's sponsors to assert that not only were the dozen plays dated after 1604 (e.g. *King Lear,* 1605 and *The Tempest*, 1611) actually written earlier, but they've had to go through all sorts of conniptions to charge that all the dates were either inaccurate, or false.

Allegedly the work of a massive conspiracy on the part of the Stratfordians, those devils. But Ogburn and Ward don't stop there. In addition to changing the dates around to fit into de Vere's lifetime, they have also made much of the White and Wright plays that were registered around 1590, titled "King Leire" and "Leare," suggesting that since Shakespeare hadn't registered anything that early (a good argument) he couldn't have written *King Lear*. But again, there's no evidence to connect de Vere to either play, regardless.

There are other distinct problems with some of the specifics of Charlton Ogburn's charges surrounding all this supposed chicanery: particularly in regards to *Troilus and Cressida*. This play was first staged in 1603, and not published until 1609 by Bonian and Walley. The editors, in their accompanying epistle say of the author "believe this, that when he is gone and his comedies out of sale you will scramble for them and set up a new English Inquisition." This is awkward for de Vere, since Bonian and Walley are clearly asserting that the author was still alive. Finally, Irvin Matus observes: "[de Vere], in writing plays for the public stage in his mature years (perhaps even acting in them 'for sport'), was thus willing to defy convention—though not so far as to put his name to them. And, as a young man he was so bold as to publish his own verse. Why did [de Vere], or his supposed literary executors, make no effort to collect and publish his poetry and court comedy in the more relaxed climate of the 1590's? If we grant that [de Vere] might have refrained from publishing these works in life, why did not his purported literary executors do him this good office in death?"

The same could be said for Shakespeare himself, of course, because nothing was done with "his" plays for seven years after his death, until the publication of the Folio. De Vereians have made much of the lack of elegy for Shakespeare by his contemporaries, particularly upon his death: a good argument. But this is even more true of de Vere himself. And here the argument that de Vere needed to conceal his identity during his lifetime falls flat upon his death. That would have been the time of times to declare his immortality, not bury it.

Had Edward de Vere, the 17th Earl of Oxford, been a man of the people (he was not), he might have made a better case as the Bard.

Had the Shakespearean classics been more like the plays of Sir Philip Sidney—of and about courtly subjects—again a better case might have been made. Especially since much of the de Vereians' case is premised on the Earl's noble upbringing and presence (albeit unwanted) in the court. But again, had "Shakespeare" written only for the nobility, he, like Sidney, would have been long since forgotten. "Shakespeare," by his writing, was a man of the people.

There is no evidence at all that the Earl of Oxford troubled himself to mingle with the masses, the "groundlings" that were the backbone of theatergoers in the Elizabethan era. (Unlike today, when only students, Yuppies and the upper middle class seem drawn to the theater, and everyone else goes to the movies). Edward de Vere may have been a "patron" of the arts. But as an artist himself, there is virtually no plausible evidence Edward de Vere was anything more serious than a dabbler. No, for the best candidate of all for true authorship of the Works, one must look elsewhere, south and east of London, towards Kent, and the ancient city of Canterbury . . .

PART TWO

THE SPY WHO COULDN'T COME HOME

Chapter Nine

A Canterbury Tale

What Mark Twain, Ralph Waldo Emerson, Henry James, Samuel Coleridge and the other literary stalwarts quoted earlier did not know, could not know at the time they so emphatically expressed their doubts regarding Shakespeare's authorship, was the answer as to who, if not Shakespeare, could have written the great works in the Canon.

One reason for so much doubt and speculation over the centuries was that, while openly questioning the official position of Academe regarding Shakespeare's role, they neglected to question the official government position regarding the fate of another writer of tremendous talent and potential.

Over the past century virtually mountains of evidence have been quietly accruing pointing in an entirely different direction from those previously considered, towards the one man who should have been the obvious choice to begin with: the outspoken young poet and free thinker from Canterbury and Cambridge University, Christopher Marlowe. Marlowe was, in the words of critic John Ingram, "this youthful ringleader of free thought, this champion of revolutionary upheaval against countless centuries of mental oppression." He was truly "the Muse's Darling," as his friend and contemporary Thomas Peele so affectionately called him.

Christopher Marlowe was born in Canterbury, Kent, on February 26, 1564, the same year the actor Shakespeare and astronomer Galileo Galileus were born. Marlowe, like Shakespeare, came of humble origins. He was the eldest son of shoemaker John Marley (also known as Morley, or also, for the Arthurian-minded, Merlin) who was, according to Kentian scholar and biographer William Urry, much more than a shoemaker. John Marley was a consummate storyteller as well, although he may have been abusive and a drunkard. But someone certainly instilled in his son a love of poetry and the theater early on, unlike Shakespeare, whose illiterate family displayed and revealed not the slightest aspiration towards learning and literature. Also unlike Shakespeare, Marlowe sought and received a world-class education.

Whoever inspired him as a child, by age fifteen Christopher was learned and gifted enough to win a scholarship to the King's School, which he entered on January 14, 1579. This was the grammar and secondary school established by Henry VIII, after abolishing the previously existing monasteries in Canterbury. There, while Will Shakespeare was learning to carve mutton in Stratford, Kit Marlowe was learning the literary classics, Latin, Greek, poetry, letter-writing, and calligraphy. He sang in the Cathedral boys choir, and then began writing and performing plays, which practice he continued at Corpus Christi College in Cambridge, beginning in December, 1580.

At Cambridge, Kit was renowned even from his earliest days as a ringleader of the "University Wits," and a gifted young playwright, and scholar. He translated the ribald works of Ovid as an undergraduate—so prevalent in the Shakespearean Canon and pointedly unavailable to Stratford schoolboys. Marlowe made the acquaintance of his lifelong friend Thomas Nash, earned his Bachelor of Arts degree in 1584, and his Master's degree in 1587. The latter was held up when he was expelled from the university on suspicion of treason, for traveling to France (at the behest of his government, as it turned out) in a time when xenophobia and paranoia were running rampant throughout Europe. This episode marked the beginning of a brief, fascinating, and troubled relationship between the young scholar and the Queen's counselors that would ultimately lead to his apparent demise.

Marlowe was multi-lingual and world-traveled. He strove to be a gentleman and saw himself as such (contrary to his deliberate characterization as a low-life by most historians). He became a favorite of Queen Elizabeth's Secretary of State Lord Burghley and Sir Frances Walsingham, her head of security. He performed invaluable services for the Queen as an intelligence agent in France, at a time when Spain was mounting its vast European-supported Armada against her. He had numerous friends and contacts from the lowest to the highest levels of Elizabethan society, including Bacon. But most importantly, he was unquestionably a poet of the highest caliber, the poet, who—by 1593 at the age of twenty nine—stood unchallenged as England's most celebrated playwright. It was Marlowe who invented the blank verse which made a new genre of theater so popular. And it was he who wrote the first English history play (which became a popular genre in itself): *Edward II*. Were it not for a single confounding circumstance, Kit Marlowe would have been the obvious candidate for authorship all along, truly the only candidate. Here's a description of the gentleman (at age 26):

His status was of middle length, Well jointed of a good strength, Silken writs report to us Was that Trojan, Troilus. For he was of comely visage, And his manners of courteous usage His hair in curled locks hung down, And well I wot, the color was nut-brown, And yet it was full bright and sheen. Such wore Paris, I ween, When he sailed to Grecia To fetch the fair Helena. His front (forehead) was of a silver hue, Powdered thick with veins of blue. His eyes were luminous, Crystalline and beauteous, Gray and sparkling like the stars, When the day her light up spars. His cheeks like the lilies white, Or as Luna being bright, And yet comely thereupon Was shadowed color vermilion, That gazers all woulden suppose How the lily and the rose Did make war each with other, Which should be above another. His suercoat was of satin blue,

Like unto a lover true. His hose were guarded (trimmed) along With many a broad velvet thong. His cloak grew large and side (wide) And a fair whinyard by his side, The pommel gilt. And on his head He had a bonnet, color red. An alder liefer swain I ween, On the barge there was not seen, And then thus he 'gan tell, What in Cambridge to a scholar befell.

(As described by Marlowe's friend and colleague, Thomas Nash)

The main obstacle to Marlowe's serious consideration was the inconvenient assumption that he was dead by the time most of the plays were written. Granted, this is a bit awkward. Yet compelling evidence suggests that, as Mark Twain once said about himself, "rumors of (his) demise have been greatly exaggerated." The reader should note that from this point forward, this author will be building a case based not on surmise, but on evidence, both factual and circumstantial, that Kit Marlowe was alive, well, and writing the great plays attributed to Shakespeare from a place of permanent exile in Europe, primarily Italy, where so many of the plays were set. Should a good detective set his mind to it, I believe he would find (and the reader will agree), upon examining the evidence, that the case for Marlowe is far stronger than for any other candidate, especially Shakespeare. This requires an open mind to be sure: a willingness to read between the lines, read the lines themselves with new awareness, and treat this greatest of literary mysteries as a piece of detective work. All the reader need do is follow along and visualize the picture, as we apply simple logic to assemble the pieces of the puzzle that already lie before us.

What all of this is leading to, of course, is that Marlowe did not really die in Deptford. The evidence, the logic of what clearly must have happened is too compelling to dismiss: that he or his supporters (among them Francis Walsingham's young cousin Sir Thomas) staged his "death" to avoid an impending and inevitable conviction and execution by the Star Chamber. He'd already been arrested and was out on bail on charges of heresy. There was no defense to this charge, and the penalty was always death. Who would not do the same, under the same circumstances, other than a fool or a martyr? It would be foolhardy, given the opportunity to escape (which he'd plainly been given, probably by Burghley himself) to act any differently. And if he survived, as the evidence strongly indicates that he did, then all of those plays and sonnets so suspiciously similar to his own works, so fraught with his own lines and images, feelings and experiences, must be seen in an entirely different light.

The truth would have been known all along, had anyone before Sir George Greenwood bothered to look objectively at evidence in plain view in the historical record. There is one single witness from the time, and one only, who could (and did) testify as to the relative merits of the claims of Shakespeare versus those for Christopher Marlowe, who died branded as "he that will forget God." That witness's name was Elizabeth Tudor, Queen of England.

The play in question was *Richard II*. The occasion was February, 1601, on the anniversary of the execution of Mary Queen of Scots by Queen Elizabeth. A deputation of loyalists faithful to Robert Devereaux, the Earl of Essex, led by Jocelyn Percy the latest Earl of Northumberland, sponsored a performance of this now "old" play at the Globe, apparently in hopes of stirring up an insurrection. They were only too successful, and the next day the Queen ordered the arrest of historian Sir John Hayward, believing he was responsible for a particularly onerous deposition scene in the play. Lord Essex himself was arrested shortly thereafter. Most strangely, William Shakespeare, the self-described "author" of the play who had placed his name on the third Quarto in 1598, was not arrested! Here is a quote from the actual deposition regarding this apparent clemency when other heads were rolling, as recorded by the Queen's own jurist Sir William Lambarde, "in regards to the evidence against Essex, including the play book in question."

"So her Majestie fell upon the reign of King Richard II" [the play book] "saying, 'I am Richard II. know ye not that?'

W. L. 'such a wicked imagination was determined and attempted by a most unkind Gent. the most adorned creature that ever your Majestie made.'

Her Majestie. 'He that will forget God, will also forget his benefactors; this trajedy was played 40 (tie) times in open streets and houses.'"

This is a clear statement by the Queen that she knew Marlowe to be author of the play. Lambarde's references to "the most adorned creature that ever your Majestie made," could not possibly have meant Shakespeare, who never appeared at court or received any known benefits from the Queen. Not so Marlowe, who was a favorite and prodigy of both Lord William Cecil Burghley and Sir Francis Walsingham, the Queen's two most trusted and powerful counselors.

Her comment "He that will forget God" was a direct and distinct reference to Marlowe's indictment by the Star Chamber for heresy. Marlowe, the outspoken free-thinker, was the only playwright of the Elizabethan era ever accused of being an atheist. Elizabeth also spoke in the present tense about Marlowe, and despite her annoyance with him revealed that Marlowe's exile had supporters at the highest level: "his benefactors," including both Walsinghams and Lord Burghley. It is in the record.

Christopher Marlowe's influence is found throughout the Canon. There is a note of wonder that sometimes slips through, even from the most learned of Shakespearean scholars. As E.K. Chambers put it in his notes on the authorship of the Sonnets, "Marlowe's death in 1593 probably puts him out of the question." For once we can embrace that ubiquitous word "probably." The first person to actually raise the question of Marlowe as Shakespeare was the Shakespearean biographer F. G. Fleay, who in his *Shakespeare Manual* (1876) complained that he "did not think it possible to separate Shakespeare's work from Marlowe."

Wilbur Gleason Ziegler took it one step further in his 1895 novel, *It was Marlowe*. But that was dismissed as fiction, and after the silencing of Greenwood the issue wasn't raised again until 1923, when American writer Archie Webster wrote in the National Review that Christopher Marlowe was in fact the author of the entire Shakespeare Canon. Webster wrote that Shakespeare, as one of 16 partners of the Blackfriars Theater company, began his usurping ways with the play *Richard II* and others thereafter, putting his name on them. Webster was the first to make this claim openly. Regrettably, no one listened.

Marlowe, interestingly, had several things in common with that other contender for the authorship, Edward de Vere. Both had Burghley's sponsorship. Both traveled in Europe, except that Marlowe studied and served as an agent of the Queen's government while de Vere's principal interest, upon his return, was to show off all the continental fashions and accessories he'd acquired. (As for Shakespeare, he never went anywhere.) De Vere and Marlowe also had in common the disfavor of the Queen—Marlowe for his views, and de Vere for being an irresponsible gadabout. Both men attempted to regain her good graces. Marlowe served faithfully in Rheims, France, nearly losing his master's degree in the process, and needed the Privy Council's assistance to regain it while in service of the Queen. De Vere, on the other hand, attempted to double cross Her Majesty by taking up with the Catholic rebellion. Then when caught, he immediately turned on his erstwhile friends Parsons and

Campion and betrayed them, claiming he was the Queen's man all along.

In his book *Shakespeare, In Fac*t, Irwin Matus devoted most of his attention to the refutation of the claims of the de Vereian ("Oxfordian") school. Aside from a warm compliment in his introduction regarding Marlowe's wonderful tragic play *Dr. Faustus*, he gave Marlowe no further thought or mention. One can only wonder how he and other biographers might have responded, had Marlowe returned from the "grave."

Christopher Marlowe's own candle was to flicker only briefly, if brightly, before being snuffed. Not until soon after his "death," did poems and plays began to be produced and published, at first anonymously, but later on attributed to one "W. S.," and then more boldly, "William Shakespeare." And so it came to pass that Marlowe was all but forgotten, relegated to the status of a footnote in English literary history, while Shakespeare's name was elevated to the honored stature of a literary deity.

It was around the time Will Shakespeare ditched his young family in Stratford and moved to London to make his fortune, that Kit Marlowe went on leave from school to do dangerous reconnaissance work for Francis Walsingham and the Queen of England in Rheims, France. No one knows for sure what or why, but one clue is that Lord Burghley, legal guardian to the Earl of Southampton to whom seventeen sonnets were dedicated, was also Chancellor of the University of Cambridge at the time.

Marlowe was well known by then, consistently performing near the top of his class. Marlowe biographer A. D. Wraight believes that it was Burghley, also a member of the Privy Council, who probably recruited his brash young student, perhaps as an alternative to punishment for Marlowe's many and famed student hijinks, among them the then-outrageous production of his student play, *Dido, Queen of Carthage*.

Burghley would have sent Kit to work for Walsingham, who had developed a vast network of spies to infiltrate the Queen's Catholic enemies and foil their numerous attempts, at the time, to assassinate her and retake the throne, with the assistance of the Spanish and their Armada.

Young Kit returned from France with sufficient good marks from Sir Francis to win the Queen's approval. Even so it required a letter from the Privy Council to the university deans to get Marlowe reinstated and his degree granted. Here is the letter, from the British Public Records Office in London:

Whereas it was reported that Christopher Marlowe was determined to have gone beyond the seas to Rheims and there remain, their Lordships thought good to certify that he behaved himself orderly and discreetly whereby he had done her Majesty good service, and deserved to be rewarded for his faithful dealing. Their Lordships request that the rumour thereof should be allayed by all possible means and that he should be furthered in the degree he was to take this next Commencement; because it was not her Majesty's pleasure that anyone employed as he had been in matters touching the benefit of his country should be defamed by those ignorant in the affairs he went about.

This extraordinary document was found in the minutes of the Privy Council headed by Lord Burghley. As Chancellor, Burghley might not have been aware of the actions of the university deans against young Marlowe until later. The misunderstanding it addresses came as a result of the assumption by the deans that Marlowe, having suddenly left school and been rumored to have defected to France, had gone to join the Catholic underground. The letter assures them that he was in fact engaged in "good service" in the Queen's behalf.

And certainly, if he did in fact "join" the underground, it was an act of infiltration, as a spy—always a dangerous undertaking in the extreme, and of course the complete opposite to the treasonous act which it appeared to be, and of which he was accused a few years later.

Living under a constant veil of suspicion is, of course, the fate of spies, but would ultimately serve Marlowe in good stead, as we shall see. It very likely suited him. He was a nonconformist from the beginning of his Cambridge years, and would have relished the opportunity to mingle with and commune with persons of other beliefs or persuasions, and learn (and glean from) their views and experiences. Unfortunately, such open-mindedness was unthinkable, in Elizabethan times. But it was a prerequisite for a mind sufficiently great to encompass and comprehend and recreate the lives of such a disparate cast of characters as *Tamburlaine the Great,* to *Dido, Queen of Carthage*, to the Plantagenet kings, to *Caesar* and *Cleopatra*, to the *Merchant of Venice*, to Sir John Falstaff, to *MacBeth* and Lear.

Some of Marlowe's biographers believe that during his Cambridge years he was asked by Countess Mary Pembroke, a neighbor in Kent and wife of one of Marlowe's patrons, to tutor Lady Arabella Stuart, then twelve, who was second cousin to King James VI of Scotland. Marlowe would be the perfect choice for the role: he was close to her age, bright, ambitious and erudite, trusted by Walsingham and Burghley, and a gifted student at the university. Arabella was James' equal as next in line for the throne of England. It was rumored that Queen Elizabeth had chosen her as successor, until Arabella's favored position at court went to her head, and she fell out of favor.

Meanwhile, due to the ongoing strife between the Catholic Stuarts and Protestant Tudors, Arabella's whereabouts were kept secret. And although her family was Catholic, she was raised Protestant. Marlowe had gained a considerable position of trust in court for a commoner, even when still a student. This proves significant. In 1921 a British historian from Cambridge, Lilan Winstanley, published a book describing

"Shakespeare's" travels in Scotland, detailing his intimate knowledge of King James and even more importantly, this same young Arabella Stuart.

Lilan Winstanley's work was panned by the *New York Times* purely because the academicians "knew" their man Shakespeare had never been to Scotland. No one questioned how he knew that land well enough to write *MacBeth* (especially given his distaste for books), nor was any thought given to Marlowe, of course, due to his tragic premature "death." Now let us take a look at that "death."

Chapter Ten

Murder Most Foul?

Official English history records that on May 31, 1593, Christopher Marlowe was murdered in a tavern brawl in the grim south London suburb of Deptford, not long after his unprecedented release from custody while still under indictment by the Star Chamber by the Privy Council, in that setting under rule of the Archbishop of Canterbury for his outspoken views on matters of religion and society. Marlowe supposedly died at the young age of 29, two weeks before Shakespeare's sudden debut on the literary scene with *Venus and Adonis*. Marlowe's supposed "murder" solved the government's problem of what to do with their prodigal darling, who had gravely offended the powers-that-be, his "benefactors," with his "heretical" views and opinions. His sudden death very conveniently ended the Star Chamber's zealous prosecution for said heresy, which would have ultimately led to only one possible outcome: Marlowe's death by execution.

The only witnesses to the crime—the alleged perpetrators—were all agents of Marlowe's own patron, Thomas Walsingham, cousin to the great spy-master, Sir Francis. The Inquest was done by the Queen's personal coroner, most unusual for a "commonplace" civil crime. And again most conveniently, the body vanished, and there is no grave. The rest of the officially accepted story is controversial, contradictory, speculative, and unbelievable. The Inquest was based on testimony of the most dubious sort, given after the fact. But the evidence that Marlowe's murder was staged is too great and persuasive to ignore any longer.

That Marlowe or his supporters had the wherewithal to stage a murder is every bit as obvious as his motive for doing so. Marlowe was a master at theatrical staging. There were twenty on-stage deaths in Tamburlaine alone. *The Jew of Malta* had to fake his own death—again an obvious albeit ironic foreshadowing of the author's own fate. That the events of Marlowe's death as described by the alleged perpetrators—Walsingham's men—seem so absurd, is probably due to the fact that they may have been left to their own devices to carry it off. Their testimony is the testimony of unsophisticated roughnecks determined to protect their own hides and avoid punishment (which they did).

Which further suggests Marlowe himself was long gone by then, to Europe.

It is doubtful Marlowe ever went to Deptford at all, and we only have Walsingham's henchmen's word that he did so. He would have no sensible reason to go there, while out on bail. He had no friends or associates in that Godawful place, there were no theaters or Circles of Friends there, or popular hang-outs or other attractions. It's the last place he would go, especially when his remaining days were so few and precious. But it's the first place three surly operatives of Walsingham would think to go, to stage a murder.

Marlowe's close call in 1587 with the Privy Council and the deans at Cambridge was a clear foreshadowing of what was to come.

The struggle between Catholic and Protestant for absolute power had not abated, in those five years since the Armada. The Catholics were still trying to retake the throne they believed should have been Mary's, and the Protestants were still vying to protect it for Elizabeth. Spies and rumors of spies remained rampant, everywhere. And as has always been the case, young intellectuals and writers were stirring up trouble, the most outspoken of whom was young Christopher Marlowe. He himself was known to have loyally served the Queen. But due to the reactionary vigilance of the Church of England's own agents, word had gotten through to the Privy Council that "heresy" was afoot, spies upon spies reporting that now Marlowe was advocating atheism (and a host of other crimes) and for him, that spelled the end.

The ecclesiastical law-enforcement arm of the English government at the time met in the Star Chamber, that bloody and charming innovation of King Henry VII. Remember him? The Star Chamber was kind of an equivalent to the U.S. Supreme Court and military court marshal all in one, but with absolute power, immune from the prying eyes and protestations of the public. The seated "justices" were basically the same eighteen Lords who sat on the Privy Council except with one key difference: when the Privy Council met in the Star Chamber or *Camera Stellata* (named for its celestial ceiling fresco) they answered primarily to the Archbishop of Canterbury, John Whitgift, rather than the Queen, who was essentially uninvited, thus exemplifying an early attempt at separation of church and state. And as it happened, John Whitgift hated Christopher Marlowe and all his fellow free thinkers, with the passion of a Taliban imam.

In the spring of 1593 the Privy Council convened in the Star Chamber, concerned by the activities of Walter Raleigh's so-called School of Night. They were especially concerned about that certain aforementioned play about Sir Thomas More, involving scenes of rioting. Apparently in those days the authorities believed people were actually influenced by the popular media (which, of course, today's film and television producers vigorously deny, despite their codependency with Madison Avenue). The Star Chamber's court officers searched the rooms of Thomas Kyd, who had been collaborating with Marlowe, a fellow playwright and former schoolmate at Cambridge. In their search, the officers found among Kyd's papers a treatise that was purported to promote "atheism:" a capital crime punishable by hanging, burning at the stake, being beheaded, or getting drawn (disemboweled) and quartered, compared to which routine murder sounds almost humane.

On May 12, 1593, Kyd was arrested and hauled off to Bridewell Prison where he was racked and tortured. Finally he "cooperated," naming Marlowe as the one who had written the offending missive (unlikely, based on its pedestrian quality).

On May 18th, a warrant for the arrest of Christopher Marlowe was issued by the Privy Council, as follows:

. . . a warrant to Henry Maunder, one of the Messengers of her Majesty's Chamber, to repair to the house of Mr. Thomas Walsingham in Kent, or to any other place where he shall understand Christopher Marlowe to be remaining, and by virtue thereof to apprehend and bring him to the Court in his company. And in case of need, to require aid.

William Cecil, Lord Burghley, who as Secretary of State knew full well Marlowe's service to the Queen, would certainly have stood up for him and prevented these orders from being issued.

Unfortunately, Burghley was ill at the time and Whitgift probably took advantage, although Burghley very likely arranged for him to get out on bail (somebody did)—an almost unheard of event. Marlowe was located without difficulty at Thomas Walsingham's house in Kent where he had gone, possibly to escape the plague, since the bubonic plague was ravaging London at the time.

Marlowe did not receive the same treatment as his friend and classmate Kyd. Instead, he was released (his bail posted by Thomas Walsingham) with the proviso that he "give his daily attendance on their Lordships until he shall be licensed to the contrary." This, however, was only a temporary reprieve. A spy named Richard Baines had already insinuated himself into Raleigh's School of Night with instructions to gather evidence against Marlowe's rumored atheism. Kyd's and Baines' testimony was the only evidence presented to support the charges of heresy against Marlowe. On May 29th, Baines delivered his report to the Privy Council, which was loaded with his newly acquired damning "evidence" as to Marlowe's "foul assertions." Among them were the following "blasphemies":

That the Indians and many Authors of antiquity have assuredly written of above 16 thousand years ago, whereas Adam is proved to have lived within 6 thousand years . . .

That Moses made the Jews to travel 11 years in the wilderness, which journey might have been done in less than one year, ere they came to the promised land, to the intent that those who were privy to most of his subtleties might perish and so an everlasting superstition remain in the hearts of the people . . .

That the first beginning of Religion was only to keep men in awe . . .

That all Protestants are hypocritical asses . . .

That if he were put to write a new religion, he would undertake both a more excellent and Admirable method.

What no one on the Privy Council took the trouble to examine (and doing so was probably not in their interests anyway) was the truth about Marlowe's genuine religious and philosophical beliefs, as revealed in the plays themselves. According to Roy Battenhouse, a professor of English at Indiana University who made a study of the religious content in Marlowe's writing, he could not have been an atheist at all. As Battenhouse put it: "The blasphemous and desperate character pictured in those testimonies (of Baines and Kyd) is most difficult to reconcile with the Marlowe who studied Divinity at Cambridge and whose loyalty to her Majesty's religion was vouched for by the Privy Council." Battenhouse postulated that if Marlowe ever made statements contrary to the interests of either England or the church, they were made in the context of his role as a spy—first for Walsingham and then later very likely for his successor, Anthony Bacon, younger cousin of Sir Francis. As

Battenhouse noted: "If Marlowe was in real life an actor in the disguise drama of Elizabethan underground politics, then words reported of him—particularly when reported by witnesses themselves politically suspect—must be regarded as dramatic talk."

Battenhouse also quoted British scholar U.M. Ellis-Fermor, who remarked on Marlowe's modernism: "Marlowe appears to have been on the verge of formulating the idea that the spirit and 'desire' of man are neither more nor less than God in man . . . The conception . . . is startlingly modern, or at least startlingly independent of his contemporaries." But the Council had ears only for Marlowe's accusers, and Marlowe was too proud, or perhaps stubborn, to defend himself.

Richard Baines, unopposed by counsel and reciting simply what Archbishop John Whitgift wanted to hear, went on to accuse Marlowe of sodomy, debauchery, impiety and numerous other listed offenses worthy of interest to any Star Chamber (then or now). These completely unsubstantiated charges have stuck to Marlowe ever since like a tattooed camp number to a Holocaust victim. What is especially interesting is the fact that, regarding Baines's most famous charge (pertaining to his alleged sodomy): the oft-cited "quote" of Marlowe's that "all those who love not tobacco and boys be fools," Richard Baines is the only source in existence for this quote. It does not exist in any of Marlowe's plays, poems, or writings. Yet historians and scholars have fallen over themselves in the presumption that this quote, and this quote alone—the only source of which was a hired character assassin—was sufficient grounds for labeling Marlowe ever after not only as a homosexual, but also a pederast, despite no evidence to support this charge and substantial real-life evidence to the contrary.

Something else historians have long overlooked is the painfully obvious basis for some of Baines's other accusations. Almost line by line many of those additional charges were drawn from a liturgical treatise of the time titled *Fall of the Latter Arian*, essentially a textbook of blasphemies, to which Marlowe had once referred while researching *Dr. Faustus*. The implication here was that because Marlowe read it (to which he admitted) he therefore must have believed and condoned it.

Which is almost as rational as the Shakespeareans' assumptions that because Shakespeare had a play on his desk, he must have written it.

Richard Baines' charges against Marlowe amounted to his compiling a shopping list of all the worst offenses a man could commit in Elizabethan times short of murder, in order to have him condemned (and thereby executed). This list, incidentally, is virtually identical to the list of charges leveled against de Molay and the Knights Templar in 14th Century France, and many other dissenters before and since. All of which confirms that slander for political purposes has been a time honored legal expedient since the dawn of history.

To further assure the success of his purpose—the complete destruction of Christopher Marlowe—Baines then kicked in a whole new capital offense, especially intended to enrage Marlowe's greatest patron, the Queen, because it involved money—namely counterfeiting.

Money was something her Royal personage took very personally, because her Court was always struggling to finance its many intrigues and her defense budget was no doubt astronomical. Baines ended his 'note' with the pious assertion that "All men in Christianity ought to endeavor that the mouth of so dangerous a member may be stopped."

Richard Baines would probably have made a successful American talk radio host or Fox News anchor, if he lived today. All in all, Baines made sure that Marlowe was a dead man. Counterfeiting alone was punishable by death. Furthermore, there was no such thing as acquittal by thc Star Chamber. Once they had their "evidence" (an accusation would do, Baines needn't have gone to so much trouble), the case was as good as closed. It was only a matter of whether the accused would be hanged, burned, drawn and quartered, or beheaded.

There were no Johnny Cochranes or F. Lee Baileys or last-minute pardons in Elizabethan England.

Two days later, Marlowe was, in "fact," "dead." Allegedly murdered in that rough south-end district of Deptford by a trio of professional low-lifes whom he knew only as his employer's hired henchmen—never the sort of company Kit Marlowe would have chosen to keep. The details are sketchy, except for the version set forth by the Queen's coroner, which was buried for four hundred years and which we will get to shortly. Basically, the official story went that Marlowe, still out on bail awaiting his imminent judgment by the Privy Council, chose to spend one of his last remaining days on earth carousing with the three above mentioned low-lifes, no doubt discussing religion and philosophy, arts and letters.

Their names were Robert Poley, a known government agent; Nicholas Skeres, another government agent and known "coney-catcher" (con-man); and Ingram Frizer, another known "coney-catcher" in the employ of Walsingham. Then, in a supposed disagreement over who should pay for an entire day's worth of libatious activity, a quarrel ensued. According to the coroner and the three "witnesses," the three men were all drinking together with Marlowe in a room in a tavern belonging to one Widow Bull. The men claimed they had a falling out with the poet, and Marlowe (known as the consummate gentleman), "attacked" and was killed by Frizer in "self defense."

How Marlowe "died" at Deptford is immaterial, since he was surely not there. But someone died, and the Inquest had to be done. Had the subject not been literally deadly serious, it might have been comical for its lack of veracity and plausibility. Frizer's 'mortal' blow was a two-inch gash just above the right eye. Unless it severed an artery, which would have caused massive hemorrhaging not mentioned in the Inquest, this wound might cause considerable pain and possibly the loss of that eye, along with some mental faculties. But according to Dr. Samuel A. Tannenbaum, (*The Assassination of Christopher Marlowe* [1928]), who gathered the opinions of several top neurosurgeons of his time, such a knife wound could not be fatal. The Queen's coroner was confident this wound caused "instant death." Yet there was little or no blood mentioned, which meant no artery was severed. In all likelihood the victim, whoever he was, was already dead.

The Inquest was hastily completed, along with the 'body's' internment in an unknown location, all in a single day. Here is how Frizer and his cohorts claim that it happened: allegedly "Marlowe" was lying on a bed, and the other three, having been arguing with him, were seated at a table side by side. They must have been very cozy sorts, leaving the other three sides of the table empty. They all sat with their backs to Marlowe, which is in itself odd considering that they were supposed to be in the midst of a brawl. (But then, "Marlowe" was lying down!) "Marlowe" then "attacked," drawing Frizer's dagger, which was conveniently tucked in his belt behind Frizer's back, which happened to be facing towards "Marlowe" during this alleged argument.

"Marlowe" then stabbed Frizer in the back of the head—an interesting choice of target for a knife blow. There were two small gashes, much more similar to cuts from bludgeoning than stabbing, unless "Marlowe" was a severe weakling. Then Frizer, trapped between the other two and unable to move ("helpless to defend himself," as he put it) nevertheless managed to somehow wrest the knife away from "Marlowe" without getting up or turning around. This in itself poses quite a challenge since he was wedged between two other men with his back to his "assailant." Nevertheless Frizer somehow managed to stab "Marlowe" above the eye with a backward upward blow, thereby killing him. Instantly. All the while the other two apparently just sat there. Presumably quaffing ale.

The prerequisite witnesses were quickly called in: 16 jurors, all good men and true—among them two bakers, a grocer, a miller, a wharf owner, a land-owner. They dutifully examined the body and the wounds, heard the eyewitness accounts, and declared "Marlowe" dead. At which point he was promptly hustled away and "buried" in an unknown location later designated as the St. Nicholas Church graveyard in Deptford. The whole business was wrapped up in forty eight hours from the time of death. No other witnesses than the jury and three men present were called or allowed.

The speed of the inquiry was unprecedented. Usually it takes that long just to assemble a jury. One point no one has mentioned for all these centuries: not one of the jurors present at the inquest actually knew Christopher Marlowe. They, like the coroner, simply took the word of the perpetrator and his two partners—the three "eyewitnesses" in the employ of Walsingham—as to the victim's identity and what had happened. The body, if there was one, could have belonged to anyone. Anyone at all. Astoundingly, Ingram Frizer was acquitted and set free two weeks later, to return to the employ of Walsingham. Again, unprecedented.

Marlowe, with the help of others with a vested interest in his survival, did what he had to do. To become a known fugitive would be folly: he would be tracked by agents of the Privy Council to the ends of the earth, and killed. But if he was officially dead he could carry on without living in constant fear of discovery. It was the best solution and the only solution. Not surprisingly, Shakespeareans cling to the official story with the determination of a baby clutching his bottle, with good reason. Because if Marlowe lives, the case for Shakespeare is mortally wounded. Why else would the idea that a man of the theater could fake his death be so difficult to accept?

That Marlowe was given the opportunity (his temporary freedom) to escape execution is extraordinary in itself. Also unprecedented. He unquestionably had friends in high places who wanted him alive. Nor would Kit Marlowe have been the first to participate in, or at least benefit from such as scheme. The government of the United States of America has an entire program that serves the same purpose. It's called the Witness Protection Program. Marlowe was valuable to his government, and to his Queen. It wasn't they who wanted him dead. For them to allow him to be destroyed and his good works lost forever just to appease a vindictive archbishop makes even less sense than a country farm boy suddenly translating Ovid and writing *Titus Andronicus* with a grammar school education and no books.

Were Detective Grant (or any other stalwart investigator) to consider the extraordinary evidence of Marlowe's survival—evidence I will get to in the ensuing chapters which has sat hidden in plain sight all these years in the plays and sonnets—and the emergence of a new, extraordinary secret government agent a year later, he would be hard pressed not to conclude that Christopher Marlowe escaped England and went on to write the Canon—albeit without recognition.

Somebody did die in or near the shabby town of Deptford, just south of London, on May 30th, 1593 (or thereabouts). But, like Hotson, Bakeless, Hoffman, Wraight, and those many scholars who've examined the evidence, even a mediocre detective would be forced to conclude that it was bloody not likely Christopher Marlowe. Who it was is another matter. It may have simply been a random plague victim, already dead, since plague was running rampant throughout London at the time. Hoffman conjectured that it was an unlucky sailor, chosen at random by Frizer and friends to fill the bill. They were killers by trade, veterans of overt and covert wars at home and abroad. To them another killing was all in a day's work.

A more interesting possibility is the mysterious death of John Penry, a contemporary of Marlowe's who had also been arrested and put on trial around the same time. John Penry was hung by the Privy Council on May 29th, just one day earlier, with no witnesses. His body, like Marlowe's, vanished, lost to history. It is not hard to imagine Lord Walsingham sending three disreputable employees to reclaim said body, and put it to better purpose. The fact is, no one knew what had happened to Marlowe until four hundred years later. All else was surmise.

The first sketchy reports of Marlowe's "death" were that he had died of the Plague. Three months after Deptford, London preacher Gabriel Harvey—apparently no fan of Marlowe's—wrote a triumphal poem celebrating Marlowe's death, full of loving and forgiving Christian phrases like: "He and the plague contended for the game; The haughty man extols his hideous thoughts," and "The grand disease disdained his toad conceit, And smiling at his Tamburlaine contempt, Sternly struck home the peremptory stroke."

The Puritans, of course, hated the irreverent Marlowe almost as much as did the Anglicans. Not surprisingly they fell over each other celebrating his demise, with references to "the justice of God," and so forth. One such celebrant, Thomas Beard, expressed hope that "all atheists in this realm, and in all the world beside . . . in like manner come to destruction." In his *Wit's Treasury* (1598) Clergyman Frances Meres, he who wrote *Palladis Tamia*, declared that "Christopher Marlowe was stabbed to death by a certain bawdy Serving-man, a rival in his lewd love." And so the pattern of character assassination and slander began, of one in no position to defend himself. This is the same Meres whom Shakespeareans use as "proof" that Shakespeare wrote the plays, since Meres mentioned his name. Meres had no access to the theater and no clue as to who wrote what. He was merely publishing a list based on the names printed on the Quartos. And with his personal anathema for Marlowe he may have been less than interested in proclaiming the truth, even if he knew it.

The first report that bore any semblance to the eventually accepted official story of Marlowe's death was from *Golden Grove* by William Vaughn (1600), who was the first to mention Deptford and the stabbing in a tavern by "one named Ingram."

The death certificate and the Registry of Burials at the Church of St. Nicholas, Deptford, stated: *First of June, 1593, Christopher Marlowe, slain by Francis Archer.* The actual coroner's report, however, was not discovered until 1925, by research scholar Dr. J. Leslie Hotson. It had been hidden all those centuries in the archives of the London Public Record Office. This document thoroughly contradicted many of the previous assumptions, but not the "fact" of Marlowe's death or the unsavory setting in which it supposedly occurred. And so the official story was all but set in stone. The coroner's report placed the date of death on May 30, 1593, the cause a dispute over a bill, the location as being a room in Widow Bull's house, and the perpetrator as Ingram Frizer, an employee of Marlowe's patron, Thomas Walsingham.

J. Leslie Hotson can be credited as being the first of the post-Renaissance skeptics to question the truth of the full coroner's report. The report had presumably been drawn up by the Honorable William Danby, Gentleman Coroner to the Queen, who signed it. Which, as one might begin to suspect, meant nothing at all, other than at some point in time, someone placed it before him on his desk to sign. It doesn't prove he wrote it. Or even read it. Let alone the veracity of its contents. In fact, if anything, since Danby was a reputedly honest man for a government official, he probably didn't read it, since it was such a risible document. Hotson found it so full of holes and inconsistencies a reasonably good lawyer would have had it thrown out as inadmissible with a couple of pointed bon mots worthy of Johnny Cochran. One wonders that the Queen didn't do the same, if and when she saw the report. Perhaps she did. She had reasons of her own to maintain silence on the matter. Especially if her own government had quietly spirited her favorite playwright and gifted reconnaissance agent out of harm's way, in order to be put to better purpose than any death could serve. The inquest was handled by her personal coroner and the entire matter wrapped up, and laid to rest swiftly, quietly and discreetly. Yet there was no obvious need for doing so—unless silence was imperative. In any case no one who was there dared question or complain about the official story, four hundred years and more ago. Marlowe had enemies in positions of power as well as friends, who knew better than to speak out. And it was those friends who may have engineered the entire sequence of "events" in the first place.

That there was some sort of a plot cannot be doubted, even if one accepts the murder as having happened, given the lack of evidence, or even a body, the dubious character of the witnesses, the ludicrous Inquest, and the secrecy surrounding all of it. One theory, set forth by orthodox scholars, is that Marlowe was murdered because he was, literally, a "man who knew too much" about his fellow free thinkers, the School of Night, led by the still powerful Sir Walter Raleigh and Earl of Northumberland. But as A.D. Wraight points out, these were his friends, not his enemies. Therefore this makes little sense, when the same goal—protection of their interests by ending the investigation of Marlowe—could be achieved as well or better by having him removed safely and permanently, while still allowing him to live. And to write. And what better way, than by the perfect expedient of staging his "murder?"

What Hotson and Wraight have pieced together from the internal evidence of the writings themselves provides a strong and convincing conclusion to two of the great mysteries of all time: what actually happened to the great playwright and poet Christopher Marlowe in May, 1593; and who really wrote the Canon of great works we've always been taught to believe was Shakespeare.

Now for the evidence itself, for here is where the real truth about the authorship lies . . .

Chapter Eleven

The Muse's Springs

The first appearance of William Shakespeare as 'sole author' of a written work came a year after the death of Robert Greene, and less than two weeks after the "death" of Christopher Marlowe, in June of 1593. It came with the publication of the long poem that had been registered anonymously with the Company of Stationers in April, when Marlowe was still alive and well. The poem was *Venus and Adonis*, which at first was published anonymously. But on a dedication page that was added two months later, the alleged author was named as William Shakespeare, who claimed in his dedication that this was "the first heir of my invention."

Orthodox Shakespeareans claim, of course, that this was an overt statement by Shakespeare, that this poem was his first written work. (Even though the *Henry VI* plays had already been put into production, a discrepancy they can't explain). Since by this time the heretofore unknown extraordinarily late-blooming Will Shakespeare had turned thirty, and his "first invention" instantly polished, this begs an important question: what was he doing up until then, aside from grooming horses, acting, and selling grain or brokering costumes and plays, to become so instantly literate, not to mention successful? As we have already seen, he had virtually no background for it at all. He was neither associating with the literati of the day nor studying at any of the universities or traveling abroad, absorbing those cultures and languages he used so freely. Most Marlovian scholars, such as biographer A.D. Wraight, believe it is the declaration of the still-living but newly-exiled Christopher Marlowe announcing his new "invention" (in other words, re-invention): as

William Shakespeare, the nom de plume. To me there is a third and much more likely possibility considering Shakespeare's known propensities and Greene's invective: that Shakespeare simply got his hands on the manuscript, learned that the author was "dead," and, also knowing the printer Richard Field (who happened to hail from Stratford), helped himself. According to Shakespeare's first biographer Nicholas Rowe, this is the "only Piece of his Poetry that he ever published himself."

Having seen the level of literacy demonstrated in Shakespeare's will it's very interesting to read the dedication he wrote here to Henrie Wriothesley, Earl of Southampton, (to whom he had no known connection):

Right Honourable, I know not how I shall offend in dedicating my vnpolisht lines to your Lordship, nor how the worlde will censure mee for choosing so strong a proppe to support so weake a burthen, onelye if your Honour seeme but pleased, I account my selfe highly praised, and vowe to take aduantage of all ide houres, till I haue honoured you with some grauer labour. But if the first heire of my inuention proue deformed, I shall be sorie it had so noble a god-father: and neuer after eare so barren a land, for feare it yeeld me still so bad a haruest, I leaue it to your Honourable suruey, and your Honor to your hearts content, which I wish may alwaies answere your owne wish, and the worlds hopefull expectation.

Your Honors in all dutie,
William Shakespeare.

This rather fawning dedication, fraught with farmer's imagery and little else, far more similarly approaches the literacy of the will than the poem itself. Which strengthens the notion that Shakespeare stole the poem, put his name on it, and then wrote (or dictated) the dedication later for unknown reasons. But he missed something important. Above the title, on the title page, there was also written a motto in Latin:

Vilia miretur vulgus: mihi flauus Apollo Pocula Castalia plena ministret aqua.

These lines are from Ovid's *Amores*, I.xv.35-6, which, as it happens, were translated by none other than Christopher Marlowe.

They translate as: "Let base-conceited wits admire vile things, Fair Phoebus lead me to the Muses' springs." It would be a marvelous and terrible irony indeed, were the thief to have been completely unaware (as his education assures us he was) that he was trumpeting the true author's signature piece, front and center! And yet, even more ironic, if so, he (Shakespeare) got away with it.

So by 1593, with Marlowe gone from the London theatrical world, Will Shakespeare was putting his name on various works, beginning with *Venus and Adonis*. Here are some of the plays Shakespearean scholars have rejected from the Canon, although Shakespeare himself was perfectly happy to claim them as his own:

Locrine (remember Robert Greene?) . . . "Newly set form overseen and corrected by W.S." (compare to *Love's Labor's Lost*, 1598, title paged: "Newly corrected and augmented by W. Shakespeare.")

Sir John Oldcastle . . . "Written by William Shakespeare."

The True Chronicle History of Thomas Lord Cromwell . . . "Written by W.S."

The London Prodigal . . . "by William Shakespeare."

The Puritan . . . "Written by W.S."

A Yorkshire Tragedy . . . "Written by W. Shakespeare."

Pericles, Prince of Tyre (the Shakespeareans later reclaimed this one)

The Troublesome Reign of King John . . . "Written by W. Sh." (Chambers acknowledges this to be "probably" Marlowe's).

Mark Twain had this to say about Shakespeare's first appearance on the literary stage:

Shakespeare pronounced Venus and Adonis "the first heir of his invention," apparently implying that it was his first effort at literary composition. He should not have said it. It has been an embarrassment to his historians these many, many years. They have to make him write that graceful and polished and flawless and beautiful poem before he escaped from Stratford and his family—1586 or '87—age, twenty two or along there; because within the next five years he wrote five great plays, and could not have found time to write another line.

(If he did, Robert Greene would say it was no doubt "doggerel"). I myself simply wonder that he didn't seem to know the meaning of the word 'invention,' as opposed to, say, 'creation,' or at least 'composition.' Or was he simply used to the nominclature of farm implements?

While the above-mentioned five Works were promptly put into production in the theaters of London over the next few years (the three *Henry VI*'s, *Richard III* and *The Comedy of Errors* in 1593-4, followed quickly by *Titus Andronicus* and *The Taming of the Shrew* the next year) no name was ascribed to these plays until *Love's Labors Lost* was published in 1598. It's doubtful that Marlowe ever intended to attribute his

Works to Shakespeare's "invention." If he survived Deptford, as he surely did since there is no evidence he was ever there, he would surely have had hopes then, and for the rest of his life, that his name would one day be restored and given his deserved place of honor in English literary lore (which to this date has yet to happen). At the same time, the plays had in any case by then been acquired by the Chamberlain's (King's) Men. As I pointed out earlier, once acquiring ownership, the Company could do what they wanted with the play. Again, there was no such thing as author's rights, in those days. Nor should we forget that, as a partner in the theater that produced these plays (the Globe), William Shakespeare, factotum, had access to the playbook.

Of the forty-two popular plays published (not just performed) in London between 1590 and 1597, an author's name can only be found on seven. And of those, one was Marlowe's, and none was Shakespeare's. One interesting note, however, regarding Shakespeare's function as play-broker. One of the people from whom he may have bought a play was Ben Jonson. In his position with the theater company at the time, Shakespeare was able to, in effect, introduce Ben Jonson to the theater public. Jonson owed him for this. Which might explain why Jonson wrote that otherwise appallingly hypocritical eulogy in the Folio. In his defense, it is possible Jonson actually believed Shakespeare's claim that he wrote those plays—and if so it's also possible that Jonson's distaste for them throughout his own career came of knowing deep down that something wasn't right about them. Or rather, their "author." Which is why a good detective might conclude that he knew all along fraud was involved. In any case, how different his criticisms might have been had he known, or been free to acknowledge that Marlowe, whom he knew and admired, was the true author.

Again, William Shakespeare was neither known nor mentioned by any other colleague or critic besides Robert Greene, during his lifetime.

Again, the only other reference to his name other than from his own publishers was the brief notation by the little known chronicler Frances Meres.

It all comes down, in the end, to the first ***Folio***. This is the lynchpin, in fact the whole case, for Shakespeare as author. Simply because his name was on it. And yet there was evidence even at the outset that something wasn't quite right with that picture. Literally. The famed Droushout engraving, the "portrait" published along with the Folio, has been proven a fraud. In an article in the April, 1996 issue of *Scientific American* Lillian Schwartz demonstrated that this engraving was actually a copy of a popular portrait of Queen Elizabeth, with a few masculine touchups and a costume change. In other words, nobody aside from his old actor colleagues really knew or cared what the old player-factotum even looked like because, at least in the role of Bard he, like his image, was a fraud. Hence the various fanciful busts and portraits to follow.

Meanwhile, Shakespeare's two old actor/partners who packaged the book—Hemminge and Condell—profess, in their epistle to the readers, that these plays were "perfect of their limbe . . . absolute . . . as he conceived them." Even E.K. Chambers, the pre-eminent historian, admits that this is "not to be read literally." In other words, it's a falsehood.

One thing even the Shakespeareans have had to agree upon is that there was no such thing as a "perfect" manuscript. Especially if it was from someone who wrote as poorly as Shakespeare did, judging by those paltry few existent writing samples. All of the Quartos (published plays) differed, in terms of the spelling of his name on the covers. There are no known "originals" at all, let alone perfect ones.

Many scholars believe that the majority of plays in that time were collaborations, even "Shakespeare's." They were company productions in which actors, censors, and others all got their two cents in. Which is why they were marginalized and notated all over the place. The only professed "example" of an actual Elizabethan manuscript in existence is three pages of the same badly written play *Sir Thomas More* the Privy Council was searching for when they arrested Thomas Kyd. It is now in the British Museum. This manuscript has the handwriting of at least three different people on it. Whether or not one of them is Shakespeare is highly questionable. It is interesting to note, however, that Marlowe's hand (he had an elegant script) is not one of them. Yet he is the one who was blamed for the play's existence.

The first *Folio* was published in 1623, seven years after Shakespeare's death, during which time apparently nobody missed him at all outside of Stratford, and there barely. It included those 36 plays, only nine of which had born the name Shakespeare (in various spellings) in the First Quartos published in his lifetime. Seven had appeared anonymously, and the remaining twenty appeared in the Folio for the first time ever, anywhere: among them *Macbeth*, *The Taming of the Shrew*, and *The Comedy of Errors*. Then there were another eight plays that did bear his name that were determined by scholars not to have been his work at all. Which means that his name on a playbook meant nothing at all! It was simply a device, used by the Company, i.e. studio (the King's Men or the Globe Theater) for their own purposes.

Or someone else's—say someone else who lived in exile, or a certain patron who may have managed the whole grand scheme.

Irwin Matus, in his book *Shakespeare, In Fact*, does a competent job unraveling the arguments of the so-called Oxfordians (de Vereians) regarding the Folios. It was Shakespeare's two actor colleagues, John Heminge and Henry Condell who first brought the collection of plays to be published in one volume. This may have been their tribute to their old business partner, who remembered them both in his will. Or maybe they, too, (like Ben Jonson?) were taken in by him, and his claims of authorship. It is entirely plausible that he brought the plays to the stage floor each day, even new pages. And according to his own claims, he may have revised and tampered with them somewhat, as actors and producers often do (presuming he could actually write, which requires considerable presumption). This in no way suggests he improved them. The "foul plays" prove otherwise.

Regarding the fourteen previously mentioned "foul plays" the scholars agreed do not belong in the Canon, author Calvin Hoffman asks: "Why is one group of plays accepted as genuine and the other rejected, when the criteria for determining the authorship of both are identical?" In other words, if the academic authorities who have rejected the eight "bad" plays in the Folio (they later decided to reclaim *Pericles*, it was so good) had any grounds for doing so, then those grounds apply equally for rejecting Shakespeare as author of the Canon. They can't have it both ways. Yet until now, they've done just that, choosing the best plays as Shakespeare's and the rest as some kind of mistake.

The de Vereians made their claim of a *nom de plume* on a much flimsier foundation—that the Earl was too embarrassed to use his own name on such trifles as *Hamlet* due to his stature as an important nobleman, which claim, as we've already seen, proves highly problematical since his name was already mud in the Queen's court.

Pseudonyms are not uncommon. This author readily admits the use of more than one. In the book world, George Elliot, one of the first female authors, took the name 'George' because no one would publish her otherwise. In more modern times, the aforementioned Josephine Tey was a pseudonym. Evan Hunter and Ed McBain are credited with the authorship of numerous bestselling mystery novels. But neither Evan Hunter nor Ed McBain exist. They are, in fact, pseudonyms for a gentleman who uses these names for "brand identification" for two different writing styles and separate audiences, while protecting his personal identity. Even if there does happen to be somebody with those names, they didn't write any books. At least not those books, and that is the point. Likewise, Mark Twain was arguably the greatest American writer of the 19th Century. But as we all know, there was no Mark Twain: the author was Samuel Clemens. Again, if some roughneck named Mark Twain had shown up at the docks in Hannibal and called himself a writer, even 19th century readers probably wouldn't have had much trouble turning him away.

Shakespeareans argue that Robert Greene was speaking hyperbolically in his invective *Groatsworth of Wit*, that Shake-scene was really a brilliant, benevolent, literary wunderkind and all the rest of Groatsworth is false. But to deny Greene's charges while claiming Shake-scene's identity (and using this as proof of authorship) is a bit like the man who calls the state police to report that everyone but him is driving down the freeway in the wrong direction. That William Shakespeare was in some significant way involved with the production of the Works cannot be denied, since as a partner in the theater company he was clearly in a position to put his name on them. But, based on the evidence, his role or involvement was mostly that of an entrepreneurial opportunist, one with typically marginal scruples.

Robert Greene's "beautified with our feathers" clearly implies either theft or plagiarism. But Shake-scene may simply have been an impostor, claiming to have written the Works with the sort of rustic boastfulness Greene described in his *Upstart Courtier*. You may argue that in any case that line of thought is sheer speculation. But then again so is virtually every claim ever made by the Shakespeareans regarding the actor Shakespeare's role as writer.

This is nothing, however, compared to the rampant speculation that has revolved around the sonnets, to follow . . .

Chapter Twelve

Sonnets and Syllepses

The New Globe Theater in London, built near the site of the Old Globe at Bankside, offers an informative tour. During this tour the guides tell an apocryphal tale about how the Old Globe and the nearby Rose Theater were bitter rivals. The Globe, of course, staged the plays of its principal producer "Shakespeare," while Philip Henslowe's Rose stuck to the old standards of Kit Marlowe: *Tamburlaine; Dr. Faustus; The Jew of Malta; Dido, Queen of Carthage; Massacre at Paris*; and *Edward II*. As the stories go, after each evening's performances the respective audiences would spill out into the streets and proceed to brawl over which playwright was greater. They also quote a line from *Romeo and Juliet*:

A Rose by any other name would smell as sweet.

The implication, they would have you believe, is that Shakespeare was poking fun at Marlowe—or rather, his theater, since by then Marlowe was supposedly dead. As the tour guides tell it, the Rose Theater emitted a foul stench, the result of excessive gutterside urinating on the part of its patrons (presumably, Shakespeare's audiences had better bladders. Or at least better manners). And with typical Shakespearean inventiveness, they thereby suggest a double meaning suitable to their own purposes. All right, let's go with the Globe historians and agree that there is a double entendre in those words, that indeed they do contain a hidden message: one from Marlowe to his audiences—that a play performed under any other name is still his!

As F.G. Fleay observed time and again, there are unmistakable echoes of Marlowe—both the man and his writing—throughout the

Shakespeare Canon. Those who insist Shakespeare was the true author cannot explain this, since there are only two possible rationales: either he was a flagrant plagiarist who "borrowed" material right and left, or he was a thief who stole the whole Works. This duplicity is particularly evident in the Sonnets. Shakespearean scholars have never been able to equate these poems to Shakespeare's conventional and mundane home-bound life, and have been forced to resort to extraordinary lengths of inventiveness over the centuries, to find meaning attributable to their alleged author, fabricating theoretical homosexual lovers, Dark Ladies and other fantasies. Always they have failed, because there was nothing in the life of the man from Stratford even vaguely resembling those images, thoughts, or persons. Au contraire, nearly every word, every line of the poems and sonnets resonates with the voice of a man in exile, filled with imagery reflecting upon his lost life, lost freedom, his guilt, his war experiences (Marlowe served against the Armada, Shakespeare served nowhere) his anguish over his condition, and his loves, from whom he's been inexorably torn, perhaps forever.

If Marlowe staged his murder, there was no alternative but to go into exile. Italy was the ideal choice for numerous reasons, the flowering Renaissance being but one, France being too dangerous, another. Again, William Shakespeare never ventured out of England. But the true author wrote seven plays strongly influenced by the environs and writers of Northern Italy, such as Boccaccio and Fiorento. These plays included *Romeo and Juliet, The Merchant of Venice, Measure for Measure, All's Well that Ends Well, Othello, Twelfth Night*, and *Much Ado About Nothing*.

There were four other plays reflecting knowledge and awareness of the life, geography and customs of 16th Century Northern Italy: *The Taming of the Shrew, As You Like It, The Winter's Tale*, and *Cymbeline*. As we've noted, Shakespeareans insist that anyone with third grade school Latin could cover this subject matter and that to think otherwise is snobbery. While Western anti-intellectualism readily embraces such notions, this author humbly disagrees, and once again maintains that to write these Works would have necessitated, if not a first rate education (such as Kit Marlowe's) at least some first-hand experience far beyond what even a genius could glean from borrowed books or passing conversations. You had to be there.

Again, Marlowe was known to have traveled in Europe, in the employ of Francis Walsingham, on behalf of the Queen. He had shown a fascination for Roman history in his acknowledged early plays, and as a true Renaissance Man was drawn to Italy more than any other country. He may have tried to see his friend Giordano Bruno, the Italian philosopher he admired greatly, who had come to England and attended the gatherings of Raleigh's School of Night (Bruno was burned at the stake in 1600, also for being a free thinker whose sins, among others, were to suggest that the Earth might not be the center of the universe, and that animals might have souls).

Marlowe biographers A.D. Wraight and J. Leslie Hotson have found evidence of the poet-in-exile in numerous sonnets, beginning with Sonnet 26, an expression of wistfulness, duty and gratitude to his Patron (Walsingham). Wraight believes this was written on May 30th, 1593, as Marlowe stood on the deck of a ship and watched his native shores recede into the distance.

Lord of my love, to whom in vassalage
Thy merit hat my duty strongly knit
To thee I send this written ambassage,
To witness duty, not to show my wit;
Duty so great, which wit so poor as mine
May make seem bare, in wanting words to show it.

He speaks clearly here of having to conceal his ‘wit,’ or his art, then goes on to conclude:

Then may I dare to boast how I do love thee;
Till then not show my head where thou mayst prove me.

Perhaps responding to the sensibilities of his own times (the 1950’s), Calvin Hoffman interpreted this as evidence of a homosexual love between Marlowe and his Patron. But Marlowe was never known to be gay, despite Baines’ alleged quote about “boys,” and certain comments regarding gay themes taken out of context from *Edward II*, a play about a homosexual king. But to write about a subject merely reflects awareness of, not necessarily identification with a subject or issue. Otherwise only bartenders could write bar scenes, only kings could write about kings, and so forth. Furthermore, the use of the term “love” was used as between close and good friends as a term of fealty, not desire. Much as same-sex Europeans today kiss one another, we have all been taught that it is a courtesy to sign a letter “Love” so-and-so.

To continue on the exile theme, with Sonnet 27:

Weary with toil I haste me to my bed,
The dear repose for limbs with travel tired.

This theme continues in Sonnet 28, on to Sonnet 29:

When in disgrace with Fortune and men’s eyes,
I all alone beweep my outcast state,
And trouble deaf heaven with my bootless cries,
And look upon myself and curse my fate,
Wishing me like to one more rich in hope,

Featur'd like him, like him with friends possess'd,

Desiring this man's art, and that man's scope,
With what I most enjoy contended least:
Yet in these thoughts myself almost despising,
Haply I think on thee, and then my state,
Like to the lark at break of day arising
From sullen earth, sings hymns at Heaven's gate,
For thy sweet love remember'd such wealth brings,
That then I scorn to change my state with kings.

Shakespeare was never an outcast, unless one wants to count his flight from Stratford under suspicion of poaching. He was the one who walked out on his family, an entirely different sentiment. And then he went only to London. But back to the Sonnets. There is a separate love theme emerging here, which we will explore further in the next chapter. Meanwhile, continuing on the theme of separation and exile, we turn to Sonnet 44:

If the dull substance of my flesh were thought,
Injurious distance should not stop my way;
For then, despite of space I would be brought,
From limits far remote, where thou dost stay.
No matter then although my foot did stand
Upon the farthest earth remov'd from thee;
For nimble thought can jump both sea and land
As soon as think the place where he would be.
But ah! thought kills me that I am not thought,
To leap large lengths of miles when thou art gone,
But that so much of earth and water wrought

I must attend time's leisure with my moan,
Receiving nought by elements so slow
But heavy tears, badges of either's woe.

Again, Shakespeare was never far from home. And again the mysterious love theme, which we will get to. But stay! Onward to Sonnet 45, in which the poet adds:

. . . By those swift messengers return'd from thee,
Of thy fair health, recounting it to me:
This told, I joy; but then no longer glad,
I send them back again and straight grow sad.

This is about messages being sent between lovers who cannot see one another. There was nothing remotely this romantic in the Bard's utilitarian life. But two more sonnets echo resoundingly with the personal anguish of the exiled Marlowe. Both reflect the sadness of an aging man, looking back at his youth. These were no doubt written in the twilight of the author's life. What is significant in the first, Sonnet 73, is the use of a Latin motto:

QUOD ME NUTRIT ME DESTRUIT
(that which nourishes me destroys me).

This motto appears beneath the only known portrait believed to be of Christopher Marlowe, painted in 1585 while he was still at Cambridge (and where it still remains). In the sonnet it is translated into English:

In me thou seest the twilight of such day
As after sunset fadeth in the West,
Which by and by black night doth take away,
Death's second self that seals up all in rest.
In me thou seest the glowing of such fire
That on the ashes of his youth doth lie,
As the death-bed, whereon it must expire,
Consum'd with that which it was nourish'd by.
This thou perceiv'st, which makes thy love more strong
To love that well, which thou must leave ere long.

This same motto, Marlowe's own, appears again in Shakespeare's *Pericles* as "Quod me alit, me extinguit." Wraight next shows us in the second of this pair of autobiographical sonnets the coup d'grace: Sonnet 74, that depicts the faked murder at Deptford, beginning with his "arrest," and "bail" and concluding with "my body being dead. The coward's conquest of a wretch's knife." All of which has everything to do with Marlowe and nothing whatsoever to do with Shakespeare:

But be contented when that fell arrest
Without all bail shall carry me away,
My life hath in this line some interest,
Which for memorial still with thee shall stay.
When thou reviewest this, thou dost review
The very part was consecrate to thee.
The earth can have but earth, which is his due;
My spirit is thine, the better part of me.
So then thou hast but lost the dregs of life,
The prey of worms, my body being dead,
The coward conquest of a wretch's knife,

Too base of thee to be remembered.
The worth is that which it contains,
And that is this, and this with thee remains.

There is much more, and many other scholars since Hoffman, especially A.D. Wraight, have taken up the cause. Let's look at what J. Leslie Hotson referred to as the "Armada" sonnet, Sonnet 107. In his book *Shakespeare's Sonnets Dated* Hotson called this the "dating sonnet," because it refers so directly to an incident in Marlowe's life: while on an intelligence-gathering assignment in France, Kit joined the British navy on board the ship *Nonpareille* to fight the Armada under Sir Francis Drake's second- in-command, Captain Thomas Fenner.

The line "Supposed as forfeit to a confined doom" refers to being on board a war frigate in the midst of battle. This is yet another location in the Canon that Shakespeare never went anywhere near. The sonnet, like the battle, has (at least for the English) a happy ending:

"*Uncertainties now crown themselves assur'd, And peace proclaims olives of endless age.*" He then with a sigh of relief proclaims: "*Death to me subscribes, Since spite of him, I'll live in this poor rhyme.*"

Wraight believes Marlowe wrote this sonnet around 1587, at the same time he wrote a little known and un-credited Armada-related play, *Edward III*. This was an immature play, clearly one of the first dramatic histories written by anyone, but it closely matches the sentiments in this sonnet. In the play *"ships like fiery dragons . . . from their smoky wombs Sent many grim ambassadors of death. Then gain the day to turn to gloomy night, And darkness did as well enclose the quick As those that were but newly reft of life. No leisure serv'd for friends to bid farewell; And if it had, the hideous noise was such As each to other seemed deaf and dumb. Purple the sea, whose channel fill'd as fast With streaming gore, that from the maimed fell, As did her gushing moisture break into*

The cranied cleftures of the through-shot planks. Here flew a head, dissevered from the trunk, There mangled arms and legs were toss'd aloft, As when a whirlwind takes the summer dust And scatters it in middle of the air. Then might ye see the reeling vessels split, And tottering sink into the ruthless flood, Until their lofty tops were seen no more."

Act III, Sc. 1, 11.152-170

What is so interesting about this passage is how strongly it resembles Marlowe's cadence and style, including the graphic imagery found in *Tamburlaine the Great*. The emotional power in the images could come only from someone who had been there, and was permanently affected by the experience. Wraight's basis for believing *Edward III* to be a lost Marlowe play is further evidenced by it being a theatrical hit, as Marlowe's plays invariably were. Edward the Black Prince (who wooed and wed a Kentian woman) was performed by Edward Alleyn, a regular in Marlowe's roles. And most scholars, without acknowledging the source, agree this was a precursor-companion piece to *Henry V*.

Both Sonnet 107 and the anonymous play *Edward III* are about something deeply meaningful and powerful in Marlowe's own life experience—a first-hand taste of war, an experience utterly distant and remote from the life of the man in Stratford, then still hoarding corn and flaying swine. A.D. Wraight, Calvin Hoffman and J. Leslie Hotson all point out that there are literally thousands of clues as to Marlowe's authorship in the Sonnets, and have cited several hundred in their books. Let's look at one more sonnet in its entirety:

Sonnet 124:

If my dear love were but the child of state,
It might for Fortune's bastard be unfather'd,
As subject to Time's love or to Time's hate,

Weeds among weeds, or flowers with flowers gather'd.
No, it was builded far from accident;
It suffers not in smiling pomp, nor falls
Under the blow of thralled discontent,
Whereto the inviting time our fashion calls;
It fears not policy, that heretic,
Which works on leases of short-numbered hours,
But all alone stands hugely politic,
That it nor grows with heat nor drowns with showers.
To this I witness call the fools of Time,
Which die for goodness, who have liv'd for crime.

Wraight cites the basis of this sonnet as being the recent political murder of France's King Henry III, about which Marlowe also wrote in *The Massacre at Paris*. But there are other clues to Marlowe as well, regarding his relationship to "Fortune's bastard" (see Chapter 13, "The Mysterious W.H.") What's amazing about this sonnet is how typical it is. It is sheer fantasy to the most adept Shakespearean scholar, desperately struggling to fathom its relevance in any way shape or form to the other Works, let alone biography of Shakespeare. But a discerning reader (or good detective) can see at once how fraught it is with the images, feelings and frustrations of an estranged father, lover, and political exile, who knows full well the implications of political murder. Marlowe, one must remember, saw his own friends suffer that fate first-hand and barely escaped it himself. There's even a reference to the heretic he was accused of being.

Researchers J. Leslie Hotson, Calvin Hoffman, British author A. D. Wraight, Canterbury author William Urry and many others have devoted their life's work to the cause of bringing justice to the legacy of Christopher Marlowe. Much of their work is scholarly and intricate, intended to prove beyond doubt that Marlowe was the true author of the works attributed to Shakespeare. Interestingly, much of the evidence amassed by Hoffman and subsequently by Wraight (*Shakespeare, New Evidence, and The Story that the Sonnets Tell*) is as compelling as any forensic evidence ever assembled by a crack investigative team. And yet, much like the overwhelming case put before the O.J. Simpson jury in Los Angeles, it has been ignored. It is my belief that after considering the facts that have been available for decades and in some cases centuries (had anyone bothered to look) the discerning reader will render a far more educated and thoughtful verdict than those who have until now accepted academic dogma without question.

Chapter Thirteen

The Mysterious "W.H."

TO THE ONLIE BEGETTER OF
THESE ENSUING SONNETS
MR. W.H. ALL HAPPINESSE
AND THAT ETERNITIE
PROMISED
BY
OUR EVER-LIVING POET
WISHETH
THE WELL-WISHING
ADVENTURER IN
SETTING FORTH

This is the dedication page to *The Sonnets of William Shakespeare*. What no one has been able to adequately explain, in four centuries of often ludicrous speculation, is the identity of the "W.H." to whom the Sonnets were dedicated. This conundrum has puzzled orthodox Shakespeareans and revisionist DeVereians alike. All sorts of theories have been postulated, none very plausible. Biographer A. L. Rouse tried to turn things around, in typical Shakespearean style, insisting the "W.H." is really "H.W.," supposedly standing for Henry Wriothesley, the Earl of Southampton. This is the Earl to whom Shakespeare dedicated *Venus and Adonis* on a separate page inserted three months after the original publication (which, let us not forget, was one week after the death of Marlowe), and a year later on *The Rape of Lucrece*.

Calvin Hoffman, in his 1955 book that offered up the theory that Shakespeare was a stand-in for Marlowe, was convinced, mostly based on the affectionate intimations in the sonnets and the fact that they were dedicated to "Mr. W.H.," that Marlowe was involved in a homosexual relationship with Thomas Walsingham, his patron. W. H. for "Walsing-Ham" is a bit of a reach in any case, no better than "Wriothesley Henry." Ironically, it was Sir Edmund K. Chambers, considered by many as the greatest Shakespearean scholar, who first recognized the identity of the "pretty boy" in the sonnets. And, as so often is the case with truth, the answer was right under everyone's noses the whole time.

For many years it was assumed that "W.H." had to be William Herbert, the Earl of Pembroke named (along with his brother Philip, the Earl of Montgomery) on the Folio dedication page. But scholars could find no connection between Shakespeare and the Pembrokes other than that some of the plays were produced by the Pembroke's theatrical company, Pembroke's Men. Oddly enough, the Pembroke heirs have had no qualms about claiming this title for themselves, without bothering to explain their basis for the claim. Once offered, credit for the Herbert family was cheerfully taken, whatever the explanation. But I believe Chambers was right all along, albeit for different reasons. William Herbert, the second Earl, had founded the Pembroke Players in 1592 primarily for the purpose of producing Marlowe's plays. Among the plays this company produced was *Edward II*, naming the author as "Christopher Marlowe, gentleman." Which in itself is important, because Marlowe was a gentleman, not a street brawler prone to attacking armed thugs over bar tabs, as historians have labeled (and libeled) him. He had to have been so, in order to be welcomed into the Court, the great houses, and the company of countesses and Earls, as he was.

The Shakespeareans couldn't even begin to explain the dedication on the sonnets, some fourteen years prior to the Folio. There is just no evidence that Shakespeare had any relationship at all with the two Earls at any time, other than through the publishers, the Lord Chamberlain's Men, and the fact that William Herbert became Lord Chamberlain himself in 1615. It was in that capacity that Herbert had attempted (unsuccessfully) to control the further publication of unauthorized Quartos. This all makes perfect sense in terms of efforts to protect Marlowe's work, and none at all regarding Shakespeare, who complained far less about author's rights than about an overdue loan of seven pounds. It all comes down to the same kind of reverse logic that allows the Stratford crowd to insist that since Shakespeare's name was on the Folio, that was all the proof necessary to prove that he wrote the plays. Therefore, since the Folio was dedicated to the Pembrokes, ergo, he "must have been" close to the Pembrokes.

Thereby explaining his love for the one named "W. H."

Calvin Hoffman wasn't the first to assume that the sonnets were evidence of a homosexual relationship between "Shakespeare" and a hypothetical lover, supposedly this "H.W." person, the Earl of Southampton. There is no evidence of this. It is simply "surmised." Recent Marlovian scholars, however, have proposed another possibility entirely: that the reason the true author of the sonnets (and the plays) loved "W.H." so much was that William Herbert Pembroke was *his own son*. Here's the evidence:

Kit Marlowe was strongly influenced by Sir Philip Sidney, the first courtly poet of major literary stature. Sidney's young sister Mary Sidney would become one of the most celebrated women of their time, educated, erudite, and literate. Mary Sidney was three years older than Kit Marlowe. The Sidneys lived in Kent nearby to Canterbury, where Marlowe grew up. Philip Sidney was Marlowe's idol early on, and certainly inspired if not sponsored Kit's enrollment into the prestigious King's

School in Canterbury. Sidney would have been the perfect sponsor and mentor for a young poet.

For seven years prior to 1579, when Marlowe entered the celebrated academy on the grounds of the Canterbury Cathedral, Philip Sidney had been traveling extensively in France, and the young page with him in Paris at the time of the Massacre of St. Bartholomew's was very likely Kit Marlowe. Marlowe's description of that event, as depicted in his play *Massacre at Paris* indicated that he was close to, or was himself an eyewitness to those terrible events, in which as many as 70,000 French Protestant Huguenots were slaughtered at the instigation of the Catholic Medicis. This also ties in with Kit's early recruitment into courtly espionage by Lord Burghley and Francis Walsingham while still at Cambridge—he knew the turf.

Marlowe had to have known Mary Sidney, whose mother was the daughter of Francis Walsingham, Marlowe's probable recruiter and supervisor in Her Majesty's Secret Service. As a known lover of poets and the theater, Mary would have been close to her father's cousin Thomas as well, who would become Marlowe's patron. Mary was known to have been an alluring beauty. She was said (by John Aubrey) to have captivated the heart of the First Earl of Pembroke, Henry Herbert, and on April 21, 1577, at the age of sixteen, she became the Countess of Pembroke (the Count was 43). Mary was the subject of her brother Philip's *The Countess of Pembroke's Arcadia* and may have had a hand in the writing of it. She translated French plays, including Garnier's *Antoine*. She was also the subject, according to Louis Ule and others, for the lady Venus in *Venus and Adonis*.

The young, handsome and ambitious Kit Marlowe would have been entranced by her. She was the living inspiration for his most famous line: "Whoever loved that loved not at first sight?" (*Dr. Faustus*). Mary had her first child in 1581 at the age of twenty, a son, who was named

William Herbert. Before then the Earl had been childless in three prior marriages and several affairs. Small wonder his lovely young wife, attracted to the budding young poet/page, would have an affair of her own. There is little question she had another affair later on with poet Samuel Daniel after Marlowe's "death" in 1593, and Ben Jonson made some sly references to her probable promiscuity in some of his own works.

Marlowe remained closely involved with the Pembroke family, and after five years with the Chamberlain's Men went on to become resident playwright to Pembroke's Players in 1592, wearing the Countess's livery in his forays about London. Christopher Marlowe would have kept the secret of William Herbert's illegitimacy to his dying day, to protect the boy's inheritance as well as Countess Pembroke's reputation. Sir Edmund Chambers acknowledges a letter that was found (and later lost) at the Pembroke estate in Wilton, dated in 1603, in which Lady Pembroke invited King James to a performance of *As You Like It*. This play is fraught with intimate references to Marlowe's and the Countess's own upbringing in Kent throughout. The Countess had a special interest in this play. And my own conversation with Pembroke archivist Steven Hobbs revealed that the Pembroke papers were, in fact, lost in a fire in the 18th century.

This supports Chambers, and refutes his nemesis, arch-Shakespearean Sir Sidney Lee, who claimed the letter was a myth since it could not be found. How typically Shakespearean, to dismiss missing evidence on the one hand, while concocting their own case out of surmise on the other.

In any case, Mary Sidney Pembroke unquestionably knew Marlowe, who wrote plays for her husband's Players. She never knew Shakespeare, the player factotum, and, like her sons, would have had no reason to do so. Any surmise that Pembroke must have bought plays from Shakespeare is just that: surmise. And Mary, a noted woman of letters, had no history of association with brokers, usurers, puppeteers, or grooms.

The most compelling evidence of Marlowe's true relationship with Lady Pembroke is found in the dedication he addressed directly to her on behalf of his deceased friend Thomas Watson that was published after his alleged death, in 1593. This dedication absolutely sizzles with personal and intimately sensual knowledge of Mary Pembroke, young Herbert's mother. Here is the dedication, translated from the Latin, in which Marlowe was fluent, and which Shakespeare "may have" studied a bit of in grammar school:

To the most noble and renowned lady, endowed with every gift of mind and body, Mary, the Countess of Pembroke: Thou, Delia, of the laurel-crowned race, sister of Sidney the bard of Apollo, patroness of letters, to whose pure embrace virtue flies from the slings of barbarism and ignorance, as Philomela from the Tyrant of Thrace, thou Muse of the age for poets and all aspiring wits, daughter of the gods, able to inspire a rude pen with such feelings of lofty rapture that even my poor self, it seems, might write above the wonted pitch of my unripe talent! Deign to accept this posthumous Amyntas as you would an adopted son, the rather that the dying father humbly bequeathed its care to thee. And, granted that thy illustrious name is blazoned so far abroad, not only among us but among other nations, as ever to be lost to the rusting years of time, or even to be increased by the praise of mortals (how, indeed, could anything be more infinite), crowned by the songs of as many as Ariadne by a diadem of stars, spurn not this pure priest of Phoebus bestowing yet another star upon thy crown but, with that openness of mind which Jupiter, the sower of men and of gods, graced your noble family, receive and protect him.

So we, whose slender wealth is but the Seabank myrtle of Venus and Daphne's evergreen laurel garland, shall on the very first page of a poem call on thee, Mistress of the Muses, for aid. And finally, thy virtue, which shall outlast virtue itself, shall outlast even eternity. Most desirous to do thee honor. C.M.

It doesn't take a NASA scientist to see that this is a love letter—from the "Muse's Darling" to Mary Sidney Pembroke, "Mistress of the Muses" and Marlowe's lifelong lady friend. The dedication to Watson is almost in passing. It slyly refers to Marlowe's own "posthumous" condition, and also evokes considerable religious sensitivity which totally belies the charge, as well, of atheism. It was a paen to Mary Sidney Pembroke that would inspire *Venus and Adonis*, set amongst the fields and bowers of Kent, where she and Marlowe grew up, and Shakespeare was never known to have set foot (which is odd, considering that much of the *Henry IV* and *V* plays were set there). Also in Kent were Penshurst, home of the Sidneys, and Scadbury, home of the Walsinghams. One might also compare this dedication to the one allegedly written by Shakespeare for his so-called "first heir of his invention." A competent forensic specialist would indeed find cause to raise some questions.

Let's take another look at the Sonnets with this kind of love in mind—that of a man for a woman beyond his reach, and of a father for a son whom he can never see or embrace, and can only admire from afar. Then you see the implications, and it all falls together.

From the very beginning, in Sonnet 1, this hidden puzzle becomes clear:

From fairest creatures we desire increase,
That thereby beauty's rose might never die,
But as the riper should by time decease,

His tender heir might bear his memory:
But thou, contracted to thine own bright eyes,
Feed'st thy light's flame with self/substantial fuel . . .

The first lines are a man's most basic wish—to have "increase." In other words, to father a child. And with whom do all men, especially romantic, poetic men aspire to have such "increase?"

With "fairest creatures." A beautiful woman. "Thereby beauty's rose might never die." Marlowe was vain to a fault. He could have been speaking of himself here. Or the mother. Or his son. Shakespeare, fictional movies notwithstanding, was never known to have associated with, personally admired, or loved anyone—least of all his unhappy wife Ann Hathaway (heiress to the "second-best bed"). In any case, the next lines reveal what men fear most: "as the riper should by time decease" (in other words the young grow old and die) all men hope their "tender heir might bear his memory." He then goes on to admonish the boy—from a distance—perhaps for childish offenses only heard about.

The first ten sonnets (and many others) are much more understandable if addressed to this mysterious son, and not some unknown homosexual lover, as so many scholars have assumed. So the relationship with the son and the mother—Mary Sidney Herbert, the Countess of Pembroke—was critical to the inception of the whole sonnet project. Even the dedication page itself, subject of so much controversy and dispute for four centuries, speaks plainly of a father to his son, wishing him well as he sets forth in his life. And telling him, among other things, that his father still lives! It isn't only the first ten sonnets, either, that speak loudly of the pain of an estranged father: (Note the use of puns, so common throughout the Canon, such as "sun" for "son.")

Sonnet 35 (last six lines):

I may not evermore acknowledge thee,
Lest my bewailed guilt should do thee shame,
Nor thou with public kindness honor me,
Unless thou take that honour from thy name:
But do not so; I love thee in such sort
As thou being mine, mine is thy good sport.

And again, Sonnet 124:

If my dear love were but the child of state,
It might for Fortune's bastard be unfather'd . . .

Lest we forget, Shakespeare abandoned his wife and family in 1587, and demonstrated no remorse, no concern or care for any of them that can be shown in his personal biography. For the Shakespeareans to claim his authorship of this (or any) highly personal sonnet, is immensely disingenuous, not to mention hypocritical.

Sonnet 36:

As a decrepit father takes delight
To see his active child do deeds of youth,
So I, made lame by fortune's dearest spite,
Take all my comfort of thy worth and truth.
For whether beauty, birth, or wealth, or wit,
Or any of these all, or all, or more,
Entitled in their parts do crowned sit,
I make my love engrafted to this store:

So then I am not lame, poor, not despis'd,
Whilst that this shadow doth such substance give
That I in thy abundance am suffic'd
And by a part of all thy glory live.
Look what is best, that best I wish in thee:
This wish I have; then ten times happy me!

Many of the later sonnets were written in the waning years of the poet's life, dealing with other personalities and other conflicts. But the whole series began with the sonnets addressed to William Herbert, "Mr. W. H." and to his mother. Biographer Louis Ule believed they were commissioned by the Pembrokes as a series of poems urging the young heir William to marry quickly and secure his inheritance as the Third Earl, something Marlowe could certainly never have given him and could only have ruined. William Shakespeare was a businessman and factotum, that is all we know of him—and that he retired fat and contented in his large home in Stratford. He was never estranged, exiled, or forcibly separated from anyone. Nor, for that matter, was Edward de Vere. The man who suffered and expressed those feelings again and again could only be Christopher Marlowe.

That William Herbert Pembroke was the son of Christopher Marlowe is compelling, but of course unproven. One very possible way to prove it would be DNA testing. Numerous Marleys (Marlowe's original family name) still live in Kent, including the prominent Marley tile family. Some of these are unquestionably descendants of Marlowe's father John Marley, and possibly his brother Thomas. According to biographer William Urry's papers, Marlowe's missing brother Thomas was not dead as presumed when he did not appear in his father's will, but turned up as one of the Governor's Men on the ship *Jonathan*, which sailed to the New World landing at Pashehaughs by James City in Virginia, in

1624. Likewise, the descendants of William Herbert still live and continue to enjoy their inherited title to the Earldom of Pembroke. And in the case of the current 17th Earl, of Montgomery as well. Perhaps one day the parties will agree to the kind of DNA testing that recently revealed the truth about Thomas Jefferson's relationship with Sally Hemming. For the Marleys the benefits would be obvious. For the Herberts, it would prove some ancient hanky panky on the part of Mary and the subsequent illegitimacy of William Herbert. But it would also entitle the Herbert family to a strong claim to the Shakespeare Canon—a far greater gain than any possible losses to the family in terms of embarrassment. After all, there were plenty of kings descended from "commoners," none of whom were the genius Marlowe certainly was.

In any case, the claim of fatherhood by Marlowe of "W. H." is far more plausible than any claim made on behalf of the man from Stratford. In summation, there is no valid explanation the Shakespeareans can come up with for the sonnets themselves, let alone the dedication to the Pembrokes, let alone the words written on the dedication page to "W. H." The man who would wistfully enjoin his son to "Look what is best, that best I wish in thee," and the one who ditched his family, never wrote a known letter and would not even bother to educate his own children are not the same man. And without the sonnets, the Shakespeareans have no case for the Plays.

Chapter Fourteen

Literary DNA and Other Evidence

Biographer A.D. Wraight has become something of a specialist in identifying "companion-pieces" in the works of Marlowe and "Shakespeare," a natural evolution from what Calvin Hoffman called "parallelisms." These companion pieces show that, having done an early developmental work on a theme close to his heart, the author then reworked and redeveloped it again later. Likewise he repeated favorite lines of dialogue or text, which would serve the dual purpose of leaving signals or markers that he, *Ibsis*, still lives! Wraight further points out that often entire works are parallel in theme, style, and subject matter. Examples would be *The Jew of Malta* and *The Merchant of Venice*; *The Massacre at Paris* and *Love's Labor's Lost*, both dealing with the King of Navarre and the French Huguenot holocaust; *Dido, Queen of Carthage* and *Antony and Cleopatra*, Dido being an early portrait of Cleopatra; *Dr. Faustus* and *Macbeth*, in which both protagonists invoke the supernatural forces that lead to catastrophe and tragedy. And the epic poem *Hero and Leander* is an obvious sequel to *Venus and Adonis*. Shakespeareans, when cornered, will admit that Shakespeare "may have" incorporated some of Marlowe's work into his own. As though this was a perfectly natural and acceptable thing to do. Which brings us back to the quote from Ovid that Marlowe translated and later appeared on the title page of *Venus and Adonis*, in which Ovid refers to "sad lover's heads". This quote perfectly matches the description of *Hero and Leander*, the epic masterpiece Marlowe was writing when overtaken by tragedy.

When a company of Huguenots settled in Canterbury after the Massacre of St. Bartolemew in Paris (1572), Marlowe's father John Marley, personally chafing at the defeat of the English by the French at Calais, surely regaled them with reminders of the derring-do of King Henry V at the battle of Agincourt. This most likely inspired young Christopher to write the long anonymous and rather juvenile play, *Famous Victories of Henry the Fifth*. Sir John Oldcastle, one of Prince Hal's "boon companions" had settled in Canterbury, not far from the Marleys. John Marley's embellishments of these heroic tales moved the location of Sir John's and Prince Hal's military campaigns from Wales to the taverns of Kent. By comparisons of vocabulary between *Famous Victories* and 82 other Elizabethan texts, particularly vocabulary overlap, Researcher Louis Ule determined that not only was the author of this play youthful, but was unquestionably the same author as he who wrote the Dering manuscript of *Henry IV*, attributed to Shakespeare. Louis Ule believes that the myth of Falstaff as misguided mentor to the youthful Prince Hal was the invention of Marlowe's father, the cobbler of Canterbury, who became himself the model for Falstaff—one of "Shakespeare's" most endearing and alive characters.

This character dominated one fourth of the scenes in no less than four "Shakespeare" plays: *Henry IV* parts I and II, *Henry V*, and *The Merry Wives of Windsor*. It is easy to see how the misadventures of John Falstaff could come straight out of the cobbler of Canterbury's life, whereas Shakespeareans will insist that Shakespeare, a butcher's apprentice in Stratford at the time, must have conceived these great Kentian scenes, lines and characters out of thin Warwickshire air, while chopping mutton.

Ule finds a solution to another interesting puzzle that scholars have been arguing about for ages: the mysterious play *The Taming of A*

Shrew, published anonymously in 1594. Shakespeareans, predictably, claim this and the later *The Taming of the Shrew* are both Shakespeare's.

They are right only in that the same author wrote both, because the first clearly leads to the second, and contains numerous lines borrowed from Christopher Marlowe's plays *Doctor Faustus* and *Tamburlaine*. In his book *Murder of the Man Who Was Shakespeare* Calvin Hoffman cites a study done in 1902 by Dr. Thomas Corwin Mendenhall of the school that would become Ohio State University. Mendenhall had developed a painstaking method of graphing the writing styles of specific authors.

He would chart the unconscious habits of word usage, sentence construction, numbers of words in sentences, word length, and vocabulary. Mendenhall had been hired by a supporter of Sir Francis Bacon, who was seeking evidence that Bacon had written the Works.

Comparing Bacon's writings to Shakespeare's, Mendenhall included the works of twenty other noted writers as well, essentially for control purposes. These writers including Byron, Shelley, Keats, Thackeray, and Christopher Marlowe. Instead of confirming his client's thesis, Mendenhall discovered—to his astonishment—that it was Marlowe who matched Shakespeare, as closely as Shakespeare matched himself!

According to Paul Pollak, archivist of the King's School in Canterbury, Hoffman had two subsequent word and scriptural analyses of Shakespeare and Marlowe's writings done at his own expense—one by the F.B.I., and the other by IBM. In each case Marlowe was proven author of both samples.

A.D. Wraight cites a much more recent study done by T.V.N. Merriam and Robert A.J. Mathews, whose method of computer analysis confirms Marlowe's authorship of *Henry VI*, Part II and III, which Chambers and most other scholars had already conceded. There's a great deal more in the way of "internal evidence." In *Hamlet*, the Prince of Denmark (himself forced into exile across the sea) gives direct tribute to Marlowe's early play *Dido, Queen of Carthage*, when *Hamlet* first greets the players he's hired to expose the crimes of Gertrude and Claudius:

Hamlet, Act II, Scene 2 (436):

HAMLET: *I heard thee speak me a speech once, but it was never acted, or if it was, not above once; for the play, I remember, pleased not the million.*

(In this scene, the author is praising an obscure play as 'Caviare to the general . . . an excellent play . . . well digested in the scenes' and so on. Picture Marlowe, talking about his student play at Cambridge, which so shocked its audience it was never performed again in his 'lifetime.' And there is no doubt about which play it was—and whose—as the next line reveals):

One speech I chiefly loved, 'twas Anaeus' tale to Dido, and thereabout of it especially where he speaks of Priam's slaughter.

(He then goes on to quote directly from the Marlowe play—the author's own sly insertion of himself into the narrative):

Pyrrhus at Priam drives, in rage strikes wide; But with the whiff and wind of his fell sword Th' unnerved father falls.

And again in *Dr. Faustus* it was Faustus, in his opening soliloquy, who first delivered Hamlet's most famous line: "to be or not to be." Except that Faustus said it in Greek: *on cai me on.*

Shakespeareans insist that Shakespeare's reputed Stratford grammar school education would suffice to enable the Bard to transcribe a few words of Latin, which, as I've pointed out, hardly qualifies him as a translator of Ovid. But Christopher Marlowe was so fascinated with Ovid during his university years that he translated not only Ovid's *Amores* and *Elegies* but also the first book of Lucan's *Pharsalia* from Latin. A huge task, as anyone who has ever tried to translate more than a sentence of any Latin language can attest.

Vilia miretur vulgus: mihi flavus Apollo Pocula Castalia plena ministret aqua

We have been asked to believe that Shakespeare exploded onto the literary scene with *Venus and Adonis* ready in hand, miraculously conceived out of sheer brilliance and divine inspiration, precluding any need for knowledge. Below is the entire quote, from the alleged first work of the newly arrived butcher's apprentice, family man, deer poacher and horse groom.

Let base conceited wits admire vile things, Fair Phoebus lead me to the Muses' springs.

Now for the rest:

About my head be quivering myrtle wound, And in sad lovers' heads let me be found. The living, not the dead, can envy bite, For after death all men receive their right. Then though death rakes my bones in funereal fire, I'll live, and as he pulls me down mount higher!

If one is to compare this elegy to Shakespeare's own grave site inscription "curst be he yt moves my bones" and still conclude they are of the same author, then objectivity is futile. Whether or not Shakespeare "borrowed" this poem believing the author to be conveniently out of the way or dead, Marlowe's friends, who knew of his Cambridge translations, would recognize at once who the author was and what his message was. That they did not speak out, never spoke out, suggests only that—

whatever Shakespeare's own intentions—the cover-up had to be protected. And again, as to its origins, the very setting, the "downs" and "breaks" of Kent in 1580, was the place Marlowe knew and loved best—where he, not Shakespeare, was born and raised. And as Mark Twain also observed, Shakespeare would have to have written this beautiful Kentian poem between harvesting crops in Warwickshire. Presumably from imagination, and also presumably setting it in Kent because for some reason the countryside around Stratford was insufficiently poetic.

In 1580, the time this poem was set, Kit Marlowe was studying Latin at the King's School in Canterbury, Kent. At the same time, Will Shakespeare was learning the butcher's trade in Stratford, Warwickshire, peddling corn, poaching deer, and dreaming of the ultimate great score, the ultimate poach, as it were. Ironically, he was able, fourteen years later, to pull it off. The poem itself is achingly Marlowe, close, but not quite as good as Marlowe's later *Hero and Leander*. Our Alan Grant is on a roll now. Look! There's more: a powerful signal, again in *As You Like It*, that the exiled Marlowe is aware of his usurper, and names him. Out of more than thirty six plays and close to a thousand characters, there is only one named 'William.' This character is a buffoon, who appears in Act V, Scene I, in an encounter with the prophetic clown, Touchstone. William is stupid, ignorant, and inarticulate. Touchstone derides him accordingly:

For all your writers do consent that ipse is he; now, you are not ipse, for I am he.

This line comes out of nowhere, bearing tremendous significance. "*Ipse*" is Latin for "I, myself." Marlowe is saying, through Shakespeare's facade, that "I am he, the writer." And Hoffman offers one more chilling clue, again from *As You Like It*, spoken by Touchstone to

Audrey—the name itself another clue, because Marlowe and Audrey Walsingham had a lot between them. Hoffman's research had not brought the story to its fullest conclusion at the time he wrote his book (1955) and so he can be forgiven for missing the significance of Lady Audrey. She was almost certainly the "Dark Lady" and Marlowe's second true love, Countess Pembroke being the first.

Calvin Hoffman came close in believing Marlowe's paramour to be Walsingham himself. But take a look at what Touchstone then says, to Audrey:

When a man's verses cannot be understood, nor a man's good wit seconded with the forward child. Understanding, it strikes a man more dead than a great reckoning in a little room.

Shakespeare scholars dismiss this as the Bard taking a backhanded potshot at his literary predecessor, whom he in no other way ever acknowledged. But for Marlowe to address his own "demise" it lends an element of anger, subterfuge, subtext, and ever-so-slight mockery of his would-be destroyers. To 'strike a man more dead than a great reckoning in a little room' speaks of something only Marlowe and the Walsinghams knew about. And of course Walsingham's hired thugs, Poley, Skeres and Frizer. What is so significant about this line and discredits the often-claimed explanation for these parallelisms by Shakespeareans as the inevitable accident of an author repeating himself, is this: William Shakespeare could not possibly have known about what happened in the tavern at Deptford because details of the alleged death were never publicized. The documents were never released to the public, the so-called "witnesses" were unquestionably sworn to secrecy, and in any case Shakespeare was never known to have corresponded, conversed or worked with anyone who would have known the truth. Coroner Danby's inquest was buried in the public record 48 hours after the killing, not to be seen again for three hundred years and more. The entire affair had been swept under the carpet by the Queen's court, and Shakespeare was not privy to the secrets of the Walsinghams. But Marlowe, of course, was. *Ipse. I am he.*

Marlowe would have taken great risk in exposing himself this way, and yet the author took it yet another step farther in the same play, inserting a character called "Sir Oliver Mar-text." Hyphenated just so. Hoffman theorized that Marlowe's friends and supporters who were shepherding his work to the publishers had recognized the danger just in time. There was a caveat placed with the Company of Stationers at the last minute: A book to be stayed. The play *As You Like It* was registered in 1600, but not published until the first Folio in 1623. And so it was kept under wraps for twenty three years until the danger, and probably the author's secret second life, had finally passed.

In all fairness, any author will acknowledge his forbears, consciously or not, with occasional emulation. It will emanate in terms of style, or theme, or a turn of phrase. This goes way beyond that. In his argument for Marlowe, Hoffman points at the parallelism of *Hero and Leander* and *As You Like It*—"Dead shepherd! Now I find thy saw of might, 'Who ever loved that loved not at first sight?'" What's extraordinary here, in addition to the exact replication of two entire lines of dialogue, is that the second line is placed in inner quotation marks. Hoffman is convinced that this was a message from the dead: in effect Marlowe explicitly quoting himself, as a signal to his play's readers that he lives on in his work.

Here are some further examples of what Calvin Hoffman referred to as 'Parallelisms'. Remember that Marlowe vanished in 1593, and 'Shakespeare' had never been heard of until two months later when he added his dedication to the already published *Venus and Adonis*.

MARLOWE: (In *Jew of Malta*): *These arms of mine shall be thy Sepulchre.*

SHAKESPEARE: (in *Henry VI* part II) *These arms of mine shall be thy winding sheet; My heart, sweet boy, shall be thy Sephulchre.*

(Actually this play has been credited to Marlowe by most scholars. Unfortunately, Shakespeare's name is still on it).

MARLOWE: (in *Elegies*, his translation of Ovid): *The moon sleeps with Endymion every day.*

SHAKESPEARE: (In *Merchant of Venice*): *Peace ho! The Moon sleeps with Endymion.*

MARLOWE: (in *Tamburlaine*): *Holla, ye pampered jades of Asia. What, can ye draw but twenty miles a day?*

SHAKESPEARE: (in *Henry IV*, *Part II*): *And hollow pampered jades of Asia, which cannot go but thirty miles a day.*

MARLOWE: (in his poem *Passionate Shepherd to his Love*): *By shallow rivers, to whose falls Melodious birds sing madrigals. And I will make thee beds of roses, And a thousand fragrant posies.*

SHAKESPEARE: (In *Merry Wives of Windsor*): *To shallow rivers, to whose falls Melodious birds sing madrigals: There will we make our beds of roses, And a thousand fragrant posies.*

(This was followed, significantly, by a line sung from *Psalm 137*, a lament of exile):

By the rivers of Babylon, there we sat down, yea, we wept when we remembered Zion.

MARLOWE: (in *Dr. Faustus*): *Was this the face that launched a thousand ships?*

SHAKESPEARE: (in *Troilus and Cressida*): *She is a pearl, whose price hath launched above a thousand ships.*

MARLOWE: (in *Dido, Queen of Carthage*): *Disdaining, whiskt his sword about And with the wind thereof the King fell down.*

SHAKESPEARE: (in *Hamlet*): *But with the whiff and wind of his fell sword The unnerved father falls.*

MARLOWE: (in *Hero and Leander*): *Whoever loved that loved not at first sight?*

SHAKESPEARE: (in *As You Like It*): *Who ever loved that loved not at first sight?*

Now five lines from another play:

"But release me from my bands
With the help of your good hands:
Gentle breath of yours my sails
Must fill, or else my project fails,
Which was to please."

This was Prospero's epilogue from what many consider "Shakespeare's" last great play, certainly the last from "his" pen alone: *The Tempest*. Shakespeareans are again effusive with imaginative scholarly theories about the meaning of these words, postulating that "Release me from my bands" is Shakespeare's way of saying goodbye to his fellow thespians. Certainly a poetic thought. But then, it seems, what he did thereafter was return to Stratford and boot his wife out of his "best bed" in order to hoard more grain, buy up more farms, rest on his laurels, and not bother to educate his children. But to one who knows Marlowe, the words leap off the page: Marlowe, if he lived, from the time of his exile and for the rest of his life, would remain a prisoner—if not in fact, certainly in circumstance. This is clearly and startlingly a plea from one imprisoned, reaching out with shackled hands not only to his unseen audience, but also to his patron, whether Walsingham or Pembroke.

If Marlowe were held prisoner in Italy, but with sufficient contacts to have access to the mails, "Gentle breath of yours my sails, Must fill or else my project fails," suggests him sending his plays to England by post or courier. It's even possible that he himself was risking, at long last, a return to his beloved England to see his son, or his lady love one last time. Or even merely to see one of his plays performed. "Which was to please" is almost an afterthought—a reminder to oneself of one's purpose as a playwright or author. Yet it best summarizes his works. As Matus put it (which would certainly apply to whoever wrote these masterpieces): "At last we see that Shakespeare's special genius is his ability to present his vision of life in a way that may be generally shared, understood, and enjoyed." This could not possibly be done unless the author was writing from the heart, from the soul, and from personal knowledge and experience. All of which points away from Shakespeare the factotum and grain hoarder, and straight to Marlowe the poet-in-exile.

William Shakespeare's purpose, if to "please," was only to please himself. Living the life of comfort in his New Place in Stratford, he never once demonstrated, in any existing document or by any recorded action, to have been motivated by anything at all other than personal profit. Not so, Marlowe. Extraordinary as it seems, all the above are but a small sampling. Hotson, Hoffman and Wraight have collected thousands of such 'echoes', if you can call them that. Some, as can be plainly seen, are downright copies. Unless these authors are the same man consciously or unconsciously repeating himself, one of them is a plagiarist. And if Marlowe is "dead," he can hardly benefit by stealing from Shakespeare. Aside from which, his plays came first.

Marlowe's known career predated Shakespeare's in entirety. Despite the presumptions of many Shakespearean scholars, there was no overlap. Shakespeare's alleged writing career did not begin until practically the moment of Marlowe's death. But mere plagiarism is so improbable as to be dismissed outright. As Hoffman put it "it is impossible for a writer of Shakespeare's [alleged] caliber to have so slavishly repeated another throughout the whole of his creative life."

And not acknowledge it, one should hasten to add. Shakespearian scholar and critic J. M. Robertson put it another way: "Such absolute duplication of another man's ideas (re. *Richard II*) would prove, if anything, that Shakespeare felt himself unequal to the invention of new ones." Robertson, on examination of Shakespeare's *Richard II* and Marlowe's *Edward II* was so stunned by their similarities he wrote that Shakespeare must be a "fumbling plagiarist" if his authorship is still to be claimed by his supporters. Marlowe was supposedly dead before Shakespeare even got started. But *Richard II*, so close to *Edward II*, wasn't written until 1595 or '96.

Another interesting clue supports Robert Greene's implication of Shakespeare as a broker. Note in *Troilus and Cressida* Act 5, Scene 4, where Troilus denounces a Greek Lord named Pandarus:

Hence, broker-lackey! Ignomy and shame
Pursue thy life, and live aye with thy name.

This sounds very like a sly, pointed, very Marlovian zinger directed by the true author at his usurper. Marlowe would have known full well the opinions of Robert Greene, who died before his exile began. However, in researching another issue Irwin Matus observed a couple of anomalies: first, these two lines appear in the second Quarto, but not the first, and there only at the very end of the play, followed by a final speech by Pandarus (see below). They show up again in the *First Folio*, fourteen years later, in both Scene 5 and the final scene.14. In other words, they appear twice. In the Norton facsimile of the Folio, published in 1968, there is a slight difference in the above two lines by Troilus as spoken in Scene 5, from how it is repeated in Scene 10. According to Norton, in Scene 5 he calls Pandarus "brother lackey," which changes to "broker lackey" in Scene 10. In the Complete Oxford Shakespeare, however (1987 edition and bearing no relationship to Edward de Vere), the two lines appear in both places as "broker lackey." And the Folio has a completely different ending, in which Pandarus delivers the final speech (omitted from the Oxford edition) after Troilus has just told him off and smacked him to boot:

PANDARUS: A *goodly medicine for my aching bones. O world, world, world!—thus is the poor agent despised. O traitors and bawds, how earnestly are you set a work, and how ill-requited! Why should our endeavor be so desired and the performance so loathed?*

This goes on for sixteen more lines, and was understandably dropped. But the above section, again, could very well be a message from Marlowe to Shakespeare, calling him what he was: a despised agent-broker. He is referring to himself as the traitor and bawd, who earnestly set to his work, ill-requited.

The play itself has an interesting history that has caused considerable speculation on the part of the orthodox scholars. It was originally licensed to James Roberts in 1603, and written the year before. The quarto, published in 1609, had two printings, one quickly supplanting the other. The first, titled *The Historie of Troylus and Cressida* bore the subtitle, "As it was acted by the Kings Majesties, servants of the Globe." Followed by the stamp, "First Edition." The second, reprinted while the ink was still wet, gave us a new title, *The Famous Historie of Troylus and Cressida.* Then a new subtitle that made no mention of it being acted anywhere, complete with an epistle claiming it as a "new play." The "First Edition," however, was also dropped, as though they couldn't make up their minds. Apparently the first Quarto was the Globe version, all set for performance, which was suddenly canceled. This begs two questions: why was the play never produced?

There is no evidence it was. And also, was the author repeating himself deliberately, or was it just an oversight?

If the author was Marlowe hiding in exile, he showed an understandable propensity for dropping little hints as to his continuing existence. He had to have harbored, as well, a great deal of anger at his predicament and towards those who might be exploiting it. But his supporters may have had some second thoughts about his speaking out too loudly on the stage. Marlowe had already written one play about the Trojan War (*Dido*) which was again referred to rather boldly in *Hamlet*. Maybe this was pushing his (or his patrons') luck a bit too far. On the other hand, Marlowe, if he lived, was unquestionably a man of action, as the next chapter will reveal.

Chapter Fifteen

Monsieur Le Doux

In 1592, Anthony Bacon, brother of Sir Francis Bacon and one of Lord Burghley's nephews, returned to England from many years of foreign service in France and Switzerland. He'd been serving as a master spy on behalf of Francis Walsingham, Lord Burghley and the Queen. Francis Walsingham, long the protector of the Queen and director of her unparalleled intelligence service had died in 1590, and a capable replacement was urgently needed. Anthony Bacon was a top ranking agent, but he was disenchanted with Burghley, who he complained had not paid him what he was owed. So Bacon aligned himself instead with Robert Devereaux, the 2nd Earl of Essex, who would become a privy counselor the next year (1593). Since Christopher Marlowe had also served the Queen under Francis Walsingham at Rheims during his Cambridge years, it was natural that Marlowe and Bacon should meet and work together.

Marlowe, if forced into exile, would have desperate need for a cover of his own, a *raison d'etre* to maintain contact with his English friends and colleagues, and more importantly, the London theater. Anthony Bacon, his health now failing, was still embroiled in desperate intrigue throughout the Continent, and would have great need of a multi-lingual operative of Marlowe's experience and caliber. Like Burghley, the Walsinghams, and even the Queen, Anthony Bacon had no reason to support the charges against Marlowe put forth by a reactionary ecclesiastic such as Archbishop Whitgift. Furthermore, Bacon was part of a close-knit family relationship connected to the Walsingham family. In 1590 Essex had just married Frances Walsingham, who was sister to Sir Francis and also the widow of Marlowe's idol, Sir Philip Sydney, the great poet-nobleman.

In the 1750's a scholar named Thomas Birch, while researching in the Lambeth Palace Library, came across an extraordinary cache of documents—sixteen volumes in all. These were the papers of Sir Anthony Bacon, proving him to be clearly one of England's all-time great spymasters. These papers revealed a fascinating character, an intelligence agent by the name of Monsieur Le Doux. This agent, who had no first name, was supposedly "a French gentleman," according to Bacon, and yet he had all the earmarks of an Englishman. Let's take a look at this "French gentleman." He obviously had some powerful backers. In addition to Bacon himself, he also had the full support and authority of the Earl of Essex, who issued an extraordinary passport in January of 1595 with the following commandment to "All Maiors, Sheriffs, Bayliffs, Constables, Headboroughes, allsoe to all Customers, Comptrollers, Searchers & other Her Ma[jes]ties officers to whome it may appertaine and to everye of them."

Here is the text of this document:

Whereas the bearer of proof Monsr le Doux a French gentleman being repaired into England for the dispatch of some necsari business intending now presentlie to returne into Germanie by the low Countries: These are to will & require you & everye of you to whome it may app[er]taine that you permitt & suffer him quiettlie to passe & to embarke himselfe with his servant in any of Her Ma[jes]ties porte without any your lette, sta, molestation or hindrance whereof you must not faile. And this shall be your sufficient warrant in that behalfe. At London the 10 of February 1595. Essex

In other words, this foreign national, this "French gentleman" was being given full freedom of access into, out of and throughout England with specific orders not to be stopped, searched or questioned: almost unprecedented even today.

Who was this Le Doux? A.D. Wraight makes a convincing case that he could have been none other than the exiled Christopher Marlowe, still paying penance to those who had saved his life from termination by order of the Privy Council from their secret Star Chamber. It was the perfect setup: Marlowe could continue to serve his benefactors with the relative safety of a secret identity, while at the same time being allowed to continue with his playwriting. We should remember that having fled the country into exile, Marlowe would have had no use for British credentials or anything revealing his true identity. In fact, any such I.D. would be fatal. And yet he would desire and seek a means to get access to his homeland, and maintain his contacts with the Walsinghams. His fealty to them was such that they would have seen great use for him. And Thomas Walsingham, at least, would recognize the value of enabling Marlowe to continue producing the greatest plays London had ever seen.

The evidence is compelling: for one thing, Le Doux was an avid reader and scholar. He traveled with a personal library of fifty six books. Please recall that William Shakespeare's personal library at his grand home of New Place in Stratford, at the time of his death, consisted of the sum total of zero books. Monsieur Le Doux, it seems, clearly had a much greater love for literature than our itinerant Bard even though he had no apparent home in which to keep his treasures and had to carry them with him. He also apparently had a greater need for reference materials than Shakespeare, who apparently (we've been required to believe) had the prerequisite knowledge to write the Canon stored neatly in his head. From birth. Unless he was a speed-reader with perfect recall who spent a few weeks in somebody's library. This is not impossible, of course. But it is certainly a shame nobody noticed. He would have been an even greater asset to Her Majesty's government than Monsieur Le Doux.

Whoever he was, Monsieur Le Doux evidently needed books for his job as an espionage agent in the employ of Sir Anthony Bacon. Lots of them. But his collection went far beyond that. Here are some of the books listed in the Bacon Papers as belonging to "Le Doux":

Junius' Lexicon of 7 languages
Junius' Nomenclature (Latin)
Nomenclature of four languages
Italian/French dictionary
Tuscan and Castillian vocabularies
Rules of grammar (Spanish)
Giambullari's language of Florence
A French alphabet handbook.

What is significant on close examination is that this "French" spy, working for the English Earl of Essex, needed a French dictionary, but not an English one! So this "Le Doux" was clearly no Frenchman. Wraight observes that the majority of these books, evidently purchased abroad since none were in English, were of, in, and about things Italian. Which, she notes, is in precise accordance with the Italian influence in Shakespeare's plays. The seven languages in the Lexicon were Latin, Greek, German, Dutch, French, Italian and Spanish. Monsieur Le Doux was therefore a serious scholar of all the major European languages except English. Which it is hard to imagine he didn't already know, since he worked for an English employer, and was taking pains to learn all those other languages. The listing of the Giambullari book indicates he spent time in Florence. This is within easy reach of Venice, Padua, and Verona, the primary settings for the Italian plays.

Among Le Doux's other possessions were an English bible and an assortment of religious books. This is particularly ironic, since Christopher Marlowe was condemned for being an atheist, despite having been a divinity student at Cambridge. According to *The Encyclopedia Brittanica* Christopher Marlowe was "astonishingly learned for a man who died at 29," who "could understand that a Muslim could honor Christ" (*Tamburlaine*), that a man could take "the whole universe into his compass" (*Faustus*). Then the Brittanica editors go on to say "his understanding of theology...is masterly." From Wraight, quoting Shakespearean scholar Robert C. Fox: "There is hardly a scene in any of the Shakespeare plays that does not contain some Biblical quotation, paraphrase, allusion or parallel." She then notes that Robert Noble has found at least one hundred and fifty references to the Psalms alone. This deserves one more recollection of Shakespeare's will. He who did not own a book, did not own a bible. The Stratfordians no doubt want us to believe he had it all memorized. From grammar school.

Let's continue with A.D. Wraight's examination of Monsieur Le Doux's personal library. There were three volumes of classical comedies:

Comedie di Plauto (Comedies by Plautus) Terrence et petit volume (A small volume by Terrence)

Terentius latine & Italalice (Terence (Latin and Italian)

Wraight again cites the *Shakespeare Encyclopedia*: "The plays of Shakespeare show Plautine elements down to the very end of his literary activity . . ." The plot for *The Comedy of Errors* as well as some plot elements of *The Merchant of Venice, Twelfth Night* and *The Merry Wives of Windsor* all indicate knowledge of the works of Plautus.

Next comes Terence. There again, we find Le Doux lugging around yet another of Shakespeare's sources. *Twelfth Night* and *A Midsummer Night's Dream* each owe plot lines to Terence's *Andria.* Poet John Davies once addressed Shakespeare as "Our English Terence."

There's more. Wraight now points us in the direction of the histories. It seems Monsieur le Doux, in 1595, was quite an aficionado of the subject matter of not only Shakespeare's life's works but also Christopher Marlowe's. Delving further into Mssr. Le Doux's personal library, we find:

Caesar's Commentaries (Latin)
Caesar's Commentaries (French)
Sallust (Italian) *Sallust* (Latin)
Tacitus (Latin)
History of the Empire (Spanish)
The Lives of the Emperors (Italian)
A work by Sleidanus (Italian)
Sleidanus on the 4 empires (French)
History of Islam by Levenclavius (Latin)
History of Turkey by Levenclavius (Latin)
Turkish history by Baptise Ignatius (Latin)
Chronicles of Prince Castrioto, i.e. Scanderbeg (Italian)
History of Ethiopia (Spanish)

Wraight notes that *Caesar's Commentaries* were "familiar to any Latin speaker." She then cites the references in *Henry VI*, *Part II*, about Marlowe's homeland district, Kent, a land of lovely rolling hills, pristine towns, villages and farms, extending to the white cliffs of Dover and the English coast: Kent, in the *Commentaries Caesar* writ, Is term'd "the civil'st place of all this isle." (Act IV scene 7 lines 59-60).

We've already seen other clues regarding Kent. We've also seen evidence, agreed upon by most academic scholars, that this play was indeed written by Marlowe. Sallust and Tacitus were Roman historians and authorities on matters of law, state and politics. Marlowe was learned in all these matters, Shakespeare none of them, and yet "Shakespeare's Roman and Greek plays, as well as Marlowe's, were filled with the kinds of detail only these sources would provide.

Monsieur Le Doux had all these materials, while Shakespeare we know had none at all.

There's more:

Tasso's *Jerusalem Delivered* (French and Italian)

Tasso's *Conquest of Jerusalem* (Italian)

Line engravings of *Aesop's Fables* (French)

Hecatommithi by Cinthio Montaigne's Essays (French)

La Fabrica del mondo (The works of great writers (Italian)

Tasso had spent time with Marlowe and his friend Thomas Watson. The Duke of Orsino, later to be found in *The Twelfth Night* was Tasso's patron, and could easily have been Marlowe's as well during his exile in Italy. Tasso also wrote source material for Shakespeare's *Cymbeline.* La Fabrica is significant because it contained writings of virtually all the great writers, among them Boccaccio (*Decameron*, the basis for *All's Well that Ends Well*). In *Hecatommithi* by Cinthio can be found "Desdemona and the Moor" the obvious basis for *Othello*, and "I and Epitea," a source for *Measure for Measure*.

According to the *Arden Shakespeare* edition Montaigne's essays provide essential materials for *The Tempest, The Winter's Tale* and echoes found in no less than twenty three passages in *King Lear*. Aesop I've already mentioned, and appears in *All's Well that Ends Well, Henry VI Part I* and *Edward III* (Marlowe).

Wraight goes on, in great detail, book by book. Another English research scholar, Peter Farey (who has a website on the subject) noted as did Wraight that Wecker's *Medicine*, also on the List, contains most of the medical knowledge of that age.

Let's cut to the chase: of Monsieur Le Doux's personal library, as recorded in the papers of Sir Anthony Bacon, more than half of the books were directly related to the writings of "Shakespeare" and Marlowe. The remainder was commensurate with the interests and activities of a professional man—an author and a spy—with a lust for knowledge that only Christopher Marlowe was known to have had. Based on all known evidence, the only lust the actor/broker William Shakespeare had was for money.

To continue with A. D. Wraight's discoveries regarding the career of Monsieur Le Doux, she points to the existence of a trunk full of papers and documents linking Le Doux to Francis Walsingham, Lord Burghley, and other members of the British espionage establishment, which is no surprise. Wraight finds particular significance, however, in the Francis Walsingham papers. In addition to being in Walsingham's employ prior to Sir Frances's death in 1590, Marlowe knew Walsingham had special knowledge of the events in France at the time of the St. Bartholomew riots, the subject of *The Massacre at Paris*. Because at that time, as I mentioned previously, Francis Walsingham was, in addition to the Queen's chief of espionage, employed in Paris as the British Ambassador to France.

HANDWRITING ON THE WALL

One obvious question a diligent investigator would raise regarding all of these issues is handwriting. Are there any existent samples of Christopher Marlowe's hand? We already know that of Shakespeare there are only those six shaky signatures, each spelled differently and barely legible. So are there any, obviously, of Monsieur Le Doux's hand, and do they match Marlowe's?

There are two existing samples positively identified as the handwriting of Christopher Marlowe. One is a signature on a will signed in Kent in 1585. His script is vivid and elegant, and he used his father's name and spelling: Morley. (his "Marlowe" surname was adopted while at Cambridge, mostly at the urging of his friend and collaborator Thomas Nashe). The other sample is a handwritten "Leaf," or page, from Marlowe's play, *The Massacre At Paris*. This, interestingly, is in the possession of the Folger Shakespeare Library. It was positively identified by Joseph Quincy Adams, custodian of the Folger manuscripts, and corroborated by F.S. Boas and Seymour de Ricci, all authorities on Sixteenth Century manuscripts. Since there are no known handwritten "Shakespeare" manuscripts in existence, this is quite a treasure. And one might say it's in the right place, albeit for the wrong reason.

The comparison of Marlowe's with Le Doux's writing is not as simple as it sounds. There were two types of scripts in those days, and Marlowe was skilled in both: the English secretary script, and the Italic script (Shakespeare, as far as anyone knows, couldn't do either). The "Leaf" was written in Italic, except for four one-word notes in the left hand column. But it's enough for a skilled comparison. Le Doux's letters are all in Italic, the preferred script for French. Yet his book list (personal and casual, not intended for others to read) was in English secretarial—further evidence of Le Doux's English identity.

But to the key point: A.D. Wraight, in a careful comparison, is convinced the secretarial handwriting of Le Doux and the secretarial handwriting of Marlowe from the Leaf, are identical, and she is awaiting confirmation from paleographers. This would be the clincher.

The rest of the evidence, the DNA, the internal evidence of the writing itself, and the circumstantial evidence in the possessions of Mssr. Le Doux are in themselves powerful, persuasive, and convincing. Tey's Detective Grant would surely conclude, again, that Christopher Marlowe survived Deptford, moved to Europe, continued his studies while serving as a secret agent, kept in touch with Thomas Walsingham, and wrote the Canon that bears another man's name.

Another interesting clue turned up by Calvin Hoffman in the early 1960s was his discovery that there was an entire line of Italians dating back to the 1600s bearing the family name of "Marley" and another line with the name of 'Merlin', another Marlowe family name discovered in Padua, Italy, dated 1521. Hoffman had a tendency, according to King's School archivist Paul Pollak who worked closely with him over the years, not to follow up on all the leads. Perhaps he enjoyed the chase too much to bring it to an end.

According to Pollak, Hoffman did gain the attention of an American reporter, who flew to Padua to follow up. The reporter looked in the local telephone directory and found "three pages" of Marleys, again according to Pollak, then flew home, presumably laughing all the way. What the reporter failed to do was to determine if there were any Marleys—a distinctly Kentian English name—in Padua, Italy prior to, say, 1594. This lapse is consistent with all of the media coverage of Hoffman's numerous investigations on Marlowe's behalf. The media always behaved as though their only interest was to undercut or block Hoffman's efforts to find the truth. At this they ultimately succeeded.

The likelihood that Marlowe spent considerable time in Padua is strong: the detail of Italian life and locales is simply too great to be gotten from books, as the Stratfordians insist the play-broker "must have done." And even during his known lifetime, Marlowe (again unlike the Bard) was a prodigious traveler, enamored with Europe, and Italy in particular. There is no reason to think, if Marlowe lived out his remaining years in Padua, that he might not have reverted to his original name at least towards the end, and sired a new line of Marleys in the process. And yes, while this is surmise, it is surmise based on evidence. Not, as is the case with Shakespeare, on the lack thereof.

Chapter Sixteen

Summary Justice

William Shakespeare's image and iconography have been considered above question or scrutiny for four centuries. Even though, as Mark Twain so bluntly observed, there is no evidence that this, the alleged greatest of all men of letters, ever wrote a single word, other than his name stamped on the title page. There is no evidence that he, who supposedly wrote with intimate knowledge of and experience in matters of state—both in England and abroad—had ever ventured beyond the farmlands of Stratford or the streets of London. Or that he, who filled countless volumes with his brilliance, ever wielded a pen except to scrawl six dubious and different signatures onto three lawsuits and a commercial farmer's will. And as Twain complained, there is no evidence that he ever owned a book, let alone read one.

During his entire "career," William Shakespeare is never mentioned at all by anyone other than Robert Greene who knew him only too well, and Frances Meres, who didn't know him from Puck, even though his name is on several of the Quartos and numerous "bad" plays.

The famous Folio, of course, was published years after his death. As Calvin Hoffman put it, nothing is known of Shakespeare the "writer," until Marlowe's official "death." Shakespeare claimed that he wrote the "first heir to (his) invention," *Venus and Adonis* immediately after Marlowe was determined to be safely out of the way, presumably dead. As Mark Twain complained, he never owned up to the deception, claiming ownership and authorship of all the plays, good and bad, to his illiterately marked grave—almost an open insult to the same *literati* who have held him up in adoration ever since. Worse, Shakespeare profited handsomely from these plays, and retired a wealthy man—almost unheard of for any playwright but common for a theatrical Mogul, while Christopher Marlowe, the probable true author, died in obscurity and probably in prison.

In 1955, when Calvin Hoffman published his *Murder of the Man who Was Shakespeare*, which first presented a strong and detailed case for Marlowe's authorship, he depicted the Bard as a willing front man lending his name for hire. And while I disagree with the notion that anyone would choose the illiterate and unprincipled Shakespeare as a front man, considering his character and known business practices, Hoffman's principal offense was to dare to peek beneath the blinders.

In the second edition of his book in 1960, Hoffman described somewhat bitterly the critical reception his book had (predictably) received at the hands of the Stratford orthodoxy. He described how the *New York Times* brought in as a reviewer Alfred Harbage, a Harvard professor long known as a supporter of the Shakespeare tradition. The academician -turned-reviewer, in his opening paragraph, stated bluntly: "To understand the implications of the authorship controversy one must first dismiss the notion that it has a rational basis." This is the Stratford hard line in a nutshell: mask the lack of a rational basis for their own claims by dismissing all skeptics as unqualified frauds (the classic legal tactic of demonizing the victim). Brook no opposition, period, because to be opposed is to risk being exposed. Scholars have spent four hundred years propping up a threadbare case for Shakespeare based on 39 famous "documents"—not one of which, they fail to mention—makes Shakespeare a writer of any kind.

Unfortunately for Hoffman, and Marlowe too, Hoffman made some mistakes that weakened his position. This allowed the army of academic protectors that had been guarding the gates of Stratford for centuries to swarm once more to the attack. Shakespeare's defenders overran and dominated the media, and thereby public opinion. All dialogue was abruptly shut down once again as to the question of the authorship: a question which Hoffman had sadly and naively believed he'd finally settled once and for all. Calvin Hoffman's downfall began with his attempt to open the tomb of Marlowe's patron Sir Thomas Walsingham, in Chiselhurst, Kent. Hoffman believed that the missing manuscripts of the plays would be there, providing the irrefutable proof he sought that they were written in Marlowe's hand. This was especially important because no handwritten original copies of any of the plays have ever been found.

There was considerable media hoopla over the event, and Hoffman was forced to undergo incredible bureaucratic hurdles to get permission from all the various legal and ecclesiastical authorities. In the end they relented—to a point. The above-ground monument was opened, and found empty. The media ran off to proclaim a Shakespeare "victory," even as Hoffman discovered there was actually a vault beneath the tomb, containing at least one casket, and other items too difficult to discern through the small opening he'd made in the vault's floor. He was forbidden from going any further, and the tomb was closed once again.

Some seven years later Hoffman was finally permitted to try again, and was able to lower a television camera down. Again nothing unusual was discernible. Again the media celebrated and the authorities pounced. The tomb was ordered sealed once more, and so it remains today. Meanwhile, Hoffman was run out of England on the proverbial rail. Like the bloodied body of Hector fallen before the wrath of Achilles, that was not the end of Hoffman's humiliation. What has subsequently happened to Hoffman's life's work is startlingly and darkly similar to what happened to Marlowe's. In 1987 Calvin Hoffman passed away, and together with his wife Rose bequeathed a million-dollar Trust to the King's School in Canterbury, the school that Marlowe attended in 1580 and '81. The earnings from this substantial bequest, yielding "at least six thousand pounds sterling" a year, was to be awarded annually to the best essay or written work submitted furthering Hoffman's continuing quest for truth and justice on behalf of Christopher Marlowe. This is the basic wording of the Trust:

The Prize shall be competitive and open to all scholars and informed laymen the world over and shall be awarded annually by The King's School to the person who submits an essay . . . which in the opinion of the King's School most convincingly, authoritatively and informatively examines Marlowe and the authorship of the plays and poems now commonly attributed to William Shakespeare with particular regard to the possibility that Christopher Marlowe wrote some or all of those plays and poems or made some inspirational creative or compositional contributions towards the authorship of them.

In accordance with British charity laws, this prize has supposedly been administered by an independent board of Trustees named by but unaffiliated with the school itself. And this committee, headed by a succession of well-known Shakespearean scholars, has faithfully awarded prizes each year—in every case to essayists who are supporters of Shakespeare. In all the years the prize has been awarded, Marlowe's supporters as of this printing could cite only one example of having been acknowledged for their often extraordinary findings and revelations. Instead, their work, like Marlowe himself, has been dismissed or buried by the Shakespearean orthodoxy, in violation of Hoffman's bequest. The Stratford gang's reach has clearly extended even to Marlowe's Kentian birthplace and schoolyard. This even though Shakespeare himself never ventured so far.

More recently, thanks to queries by this author and intervention by the Hoffman's literary executors, the School has been challenged regarding the errant methodology of the Prize committee, although strictly pro-Shakespeare prizes continue to be awarded. Nevertheless, agreeing to finally assure adherence to the terms of the Trust, the Committee has promised to establish a theater at the King's School in Hoffman's name: ostensibly to produce Marlowe's plays. If truth and justice should ever come into fashion in the sanctums of Academe, then that should include the entire "Shakespeare" Canon. Because the evidence—powerful evidence as we have seen, makes a compelling case for Christopher Marlowe, and exposes the actor-factotum Shakespeare for the paper "tyger" that he was.

Today Christopher Marlowe is remembered by a scant few scholars, primarily for a few plays and epic poems he wrote before his "demise." Some remember, as well, his reputation as a heretic, dissolute, and a spy. But in his day he was acclaimed as the "Muse's Darling," the prince of the English theater, and England's greatest playwright. Whether and how Marlowe survived and where and how he lived out the remaining days of his life remains a mystery, the resolution of which no one at present can offer, and there many never be clear or conclusive answers. Marlovians believe it was Thomas Walsingham who received the manuscripts from Marlowe and passed them on to Shakespeare and the Globe. This may have been accomplished through the agency of Ingram Frizer, the "murderer" and double agent who traveled frequently back and forth between Europe and England, according to public records, in 1593 and subsequent years as well. It is clear that Walsingham needed someone to distance himself from Marlowe. After all, Walsingham had assumed responsibility for Marlowe's "bail" in late May, 1593, and could not afford to be implicated in what would otherwise be an apparent scheme to defraud the state and aid an escaped prisoner. So Walsingham would have removed himself from the picture and entrusted the plays to someone, presumably Shakespeare. In any case, in historical terms a fraud was perpetrated, Shakespeare was involved, and he benefited tremendously as a result.

That Will Shakespeare was a broker who bought plays and put his name on them is clearly evident. He did not start taking credit for the plays in the Canon until 1598, however, first with *Love's Labor's Lost*, inscribed "newly corrected by William Shakespeare," a year later, more boldly, he published *Henry IV* as "by William Shakespeare."

Typically, Shakespeareans use this as evidence of authorship, whereas it is merely evidence of plagiarism. Four plays from the Canon were published before 1597, all anonymously: *Titus Andronicus, Henry VI Part II* and *III* and *Romeo and Juliet*. Then three more anonymously in 1597: *Richard II* (First Quarto), *Richard III* and *Henry IV Part I*.

The next year the Stationer's Register revealed a startling entry accompanying the registration (again anonymously) of *The Merchant of Venice*: . . . "Provided that it be not printed by the said James Roberts or any other whatsoever without license first had from the Right Honorable the Lord Chamberlain." On August 14, 1600 came three more entries: *As You Like It, Henry V* and *Much Ado About Nothing*. Again, all were registered anonymously with the Stationers. Marlowe may have been aware of what Shakespeare was up to by then and was trying to protect himself, because all of these plays were registered with specific instructions that they be "stayed," which is to say not licensed for publication. And indeed, none were published until the Folio, in 1623.

Anything published under Marlowe's name after his alleged demise in 1593 was probably done by someone friendly to him, quite possibly under his instructions. There is some question about *Hero and Leander*, which was published by Blount and dedicated to the Walsinghams in 1598. The 'continuation' by Chapman may have been written by Marlowe himself. Or the continuation and publication may have been done without Marlowe's permission. However, the publication of *Lucan's First Book* smells like a conspiracy in which Marlowe participated.

Quite likely he brought back this translation from Italy after some of his time in exile there. He may have delivered it to Thorpe, asking Thorpe to find a publisher for it.

By 1602, Shakespeare was taking full credit for *Hamlet* and everything else. But for the first few years, from 1593 to 1598 Shakespeare was apparently content to take his triple fees (enough to buy his New Place) and keep his mouth shut. He was not known to have ever spoken to anyone about his "authorship," real or imaginary. This was simply presumed, by Meres and by Jonson and the partners in the Blackfriars and Globe, and all those scholars since. It is clear that some of Marlowe's friends in publishing, such as Thomas Thorpe (later the publisher of the Sonnets) also became alerted to what Shakespeare was doing and began taking countermeasures, bringing out some of Marlowe's works under his own name. *Lucan's First Book* was published in 1600. *The Passionate Shepherd* (which Shakespeare plagiarized in 1599 in the *Passionate Pilgrim* anthology) was published in *England's Helicon* under Marlowe's name, also in 1600. *Doctor Faustus* was published in 1604 under Marlowe's name, with material about Giordano Bruno added. This most likely was done by a publisher friendly to Marlowe, perhaps with Marlowe's consent and instructions.

We do know that a number of Marlowe's works were registered and/or published in 1593 and 1594: (*Dido, Edward II*, and *Massacre At Paris*), as Marlowe was already headed into exile. It is also possible that once gone and far away in Italy he did not catch on to what Shakespeare was doing until 1599 or 1600. By then he and/or some of his allies began releasing more of his early works under his own name despite the stigma it bore. This began in 1599—the year after Shakespeare first started taking credit for the plays. Marlowe, if alive and writing in exile, would surely have had high hopes that he would be able to reclaim his rights later on, when he might someday return to England. He may have been led to believe that the plays would be produced anonymously—as they were in the earlier years.

In any case, Marlowe had no literary executor after his official "death" in 1593. The rule of "silence means consent" does not apply to an individual in Marlowe's situation—someone alive who is officially dead. Marlowe's silence about Shakespeare cannot be construed to mean Marlowe's consent to the Shakespeare imposture. Marlowe was a proud man, who would have done whatever possible to prevent the theft of most of his life's work that ultimately took place.

So it stands to reason that much if not all of what happened to Marlowe's works happened without his consent if not without his knowledge. It's highly doubtful that he approved of what was happening with the publication of his plays and the credit being taken by Shakespeare. But he was in no position to do anything about it. And those who saw to the production and publication of the plays and poems were clearly serving their own interests more than Marlowe's.

Even today, despite contracts, international copyright protection (not valid in Hollywood, incidentally) and "intellectual property rights," any working writer knows that it is hard enough to avoid being exploited and ripped off when he or she is known to be alive and well. It is all the more difficult when the writer is officially dead, with no executor, no will, and no legal protection whatsoever.

Even if Wraight and Hoffman were right, that Shakespeare's role was merely that of an actor hired by Thomas Walsingham to play the part of the playwright, his participation in this great fraud cannot have been passive. He had possession of the plays, that is a given. They were produced by his company, the Globe Theater and Chamberlain/King's Men, anonymously, throughout the 1590's. And he profited handsomely from the transactions. Clearly he had figured out how to take advantage of his position more and more as time went by. Note the dedication written by Thomas Thorpe to Edward Blount, with its reference to Marlowe's elemental spirit, that accompanied the publication of *Lucan's First Book*:

"Blount: I purpose to be blunt [pun on Blount's name], and out of my dullness to encounter you with a dedication in the memory of that pure elemental wit Chr. Marlowe, whose ghost or genius is to be seen walk(ing) the churchyard in [at the least) three or four sheets . . ."

This is a reference to Marlowe as a living ghost whose work appears in the Churchyard—then the publishing center of London—in more than a few "sheets" (another pun) of folio and of poetry. Or maybe he was actually seen on occasion, in the flesh!

If Monsieur Le Doux was indeed Marlowe as the evidence strongly suggests, and Marlowe was working as a foreign agent for Essex, this would explain how Marlowe's position became further compromised in 1599 or 1600, when Essex fell out of favor with the Queen. As leader of the ill-fated "Essex rebellion" Essex was himself ultimately executed. Marlowe would likely have been a spy left out in the cold after that.

Meanwhile, as previously noted, Shakespeare escaped prosecution even when the Queen ordered the arrest of the players and playwright putting on the 'rebel plays,' particularly *Richard II*, the original version of which included a scene of the King abdicating his throne to his rival, Bollingbroke. This is significant, as we discussed earlier, because Elizabeth feared just such a coup, by then, from Essex.

Shakespeare was known and readily accessible to the authorities. And while the first Quarto of this play was at first published anonymously, in 1597, he came out as its author a year later. In fact this was the first play with his name on the title page. Yet, again, it's clear the Privy Council did not consider him the author or they would certainly have arrested him. Shakespeare was already known by then as a publisher who put his name on writings that weren't his, such as *The*

Passionate Shepherd and the "foul" plays later rejected by the Shakespearean scholars. So the only reason the Council did not charge Shakespeare for fomenting the riots which occurred immediately after the play was performed, in February of 1601, is that they knew him for what he was.

And was not.

As for Marlowe's final years, one can only speculate that something happened to him that prevented his return, even after the death of the Queen. With the downfall of Essex, he may have been forced to go abroad again, or he may have been captured at last, and imprisoned. There is a record of a Christopher Marlowe in London's Gatehouse prison in 1604, which no one has attempted to verify, mostly because historians have always assumed our Kit Marlowe was dead. In any case, for one reason or another, Marlowe was unable to do anything to stop Shakespeare after 1600-1601.

In Conclusion

In summary, Robert Greene's own testimony should be sufficient, that William Shakespeare was a thief, and in the sense of his net gain, A Thief for All Time. I hasten to add, however, that this does not mean he was necessarily evil, or even criminal. He might simply have been an opportunist, merely doing business in accordance with normal business practices, then and now. He may well have justified his actions in his own mind—Marlowe was "dead." Greene was dead. Perhaps Shakspur's rustic background made him feel less than equal in the Capital, and felt a need to compensate. He no doubt endured the slings and arrows of social casting in his lifetime. He surely aspired to a higher standing, if not standard. His father certainly did, with the business of the Coat of Arms. He may even have tried to be a writer, of sorts, tampering with what came his way, perhaps growing bolder as time passed, eventually perhaps even believing in his own "genius." *The Merry Wives of Windsor*, a dismally bad play, considering its source, would fit this scenario, one which has recurred in Hollywood time and time again.

But Shakespeare could not truly write. That he could act was fairly evident, although he was clearly not in the caliber of Edward Alleyn. His company, the Chamberlain's/King's Men was the best of its time, and considering the repertoire, possibly the best of all time. (At least until the advent of women to the stage, which, let's face it, improved things considerably) But there, too, he was not preeminent. Had he not come into possession of the great plays of the Canon, he would have ultimately returned to Stratford much as he left it: a simple country businessman and player, of modest means and abilities.

As for Stratford-on-Avon, there is no undoing what's done. As a place of celebration of the art itself—of the plays—(like the newly rebuilt Globe) it serves well. Perhaps one day Canterbury will get equal billing with Stratford, although that fair ancient city hardly needs more tourists. Perhaps the new Hoffman Theater at the King's School will assume a role of preeminence as an Elizabethan theatrical Mecca.

One wrong that has only recently been righted at long last was to finally give Christopher Marlowe a place in the Poet's Corner at Westminster Abbey, alongside the other great writers of England, Scotland and Wales. Keats, Shelley, Byron: all are there. All but Marlowe until just a few years ago, in 2002. Based on *Dr. Faustus, Edward II, Passionate Shepherd*, and *Hero and Leander* alone, the long banishment of "The Muse's Darling" from this hallowed circle was outrageous. The charge of atheism that had presumably kept him out of the Poet's Corner rang increasingly hollow with the passage of time. Shelley was a proclaimed atheist, and he is certainly well remembered there, and has been since his death.

Perhaps the problem was that Kit Marlowe was a free thinker. And probably the greatest geo-political thinker of his time, if not ever. Many such were wrongly tortured and executed in a Britain that only selectively cherishes its history. Free thinkers such as Galileo and Bruno were also executed in Italy and Spain. But authorities in those countries had long since owned up to their error: the British authorities took four centuries to do so. This is doubly ironic, considering that Westminster Abbey is shrine to an entire line of kings who gained the throne by murder and usurpation. But then, in the end, as from the beginning, the rejection of Marlowe by English authority is, and was simply politics. That, and economics, as is so often the case. (AUTHOR'S NOTE: one intriguing footnote to this recent development is that the small window panel so grudgingly and at long-last dedicated to Marlowe in the Poet's Corner gives his birth year, and leaves—much to the outrage of the Shakespeare orthodoxy—his death date as a question mark.)

One of Shakespeare's strongest alleged assets, aside from the gray beards of time and academe, is his connection to folklore, his role as the Common Man (never mind that he tried to starve his neighbors by hoarding grain during a famine). This too is ironic: he is eulogized as a commoner who "made good" by academic institutions that are paragons of snobbery, who reject any scholarship or literary achievement unsanctioned by themselves. Yet Shakespeare, who claimed knowledge available only to a scholar, never earned a degree.

Whereas Marlowe did. This is the circular logic that Mark Twain condemned. Alas, the ghost of Kit Marlowe is still waiting for his credits and good name to be restored. One can only hope that, eventually, justice will be done at last. Until then, as long as the name Shakespeare is remembered so should be Christopher Marlowe. He probably wrote the plays. Shakespeare certainly did not.

BIBLIOGRAPHY

Aesop, The Complete Fables Ed. Robert and Olivia Temple NY 1998.

Bakeless, John, The Tragical History of Christopher Marlowe in two vols. Harvard, 1942.

Birch, Thomas, Memoirs of the Reign of Queen Elizabeth 1754.

Brooks, Alden, Will Shakspere, Factotum and Agent, NY 1937.

Chambers, Sir Edmund K. Shakespeare: A Study of Facts and Problems, in two volumes, Oxford University Press, 1930.

Champlin, Charles, The Great Shakespeare Mystery

Caper Davies, John The Scourge of Folly, 1610.

Eccles, Mark Christopher Marlowe in London, 1934.

Evans, G. Blakemore, et. al. Ed. The Riverside Shakespeare NY,1974.

Fleay, F. G. Shakespeare Manual, 1876.

Greene, Robert, The Life and Complete Works in Prose and Verse of Robert Greene, M.A. Cambridge and Oxford, Ed. George B. Harrison, NY 1964.

Greenwood, Sir George, The Shakespeare Problem Restated, London, 1937.

Greenwood, Ben Jonson and Shakespeare, 1921.

Hamilton, Charles, In Search of Shakespeare, San Diego 1985.

Hazlett, William, Lectures on the English Poets, NY 1968.

Hoffman, Calvin, Murder of the Man Who Was Shakespeare NY, 1955.

Hotson, J. Leslie, The Death of Christopher Marlowe, 1925.

Lewis, Roland, The Shakespeare Documents; Facsimiles, Transliterations and Commentary, 2 volumes, CT 1940-41.

Magnussun, Magnus Ed. Chambers Biographical Dictionary Cambridge, 1990 (5th Edition).

Matus, Irwin Leigh, Shakespeare, In Fact, NY 1994.

More, David, The Marlovian, "Drunken Sailor or Imprisoned Writer?" Fall 1996.

Noble, Robert C. Shakespeare's Biblical Knowledge, 1975.

Nicholl, Charles, The Reconing: The Murder of Christopher Marlowe, Orlando 1992.

Robertson, J. M. The Shakespeare Canon, 1922-30.

Rowse, A. L. What Shakespeare Read and Thought, NY 1981.

Ridley, M.R. Ed. Othello, Moor of Venice, 1958.

Schoenbaum, S. William Shakespeare, A Compact Documentary Life, NY 1977.

Simpson, R. R. Shakespeare and Medicine London, 1959.

Steiner, George, The Death of Tragedy NY 1963.

Stopes, Charlotte, Shakespeare's Family, 1901.

Tarloff, Frank, Jarrico, Paul, "Blacklisted . . . Fifty Years Ago Today" in Written By, The Journal of the Writers Guild of America, LA, October 1997.

Twain, Mark, The Complete Essays of Mark Twain, NY 1963.

Urry, William, Christopher Marlowe and Canterbury London, 1988.

Ward, B.M. The Seventeenth Earl of Oxford, 1550-1604, from Contemporary Documents, London 1928.

Webster, Archie, "Was Marlowe the Man?" in National Review London, 1923.

Willoughby, E. E. A Printer of Shakespeare.

Wraight, A.D. Shakespeare, New Evidence, London, 1996.

Wraight, The Story that the Sonnets Tell Publications: Merriam,

T.V.N. and Matthews, Robert A.J. in Literary and Linguistic

Computing "Neural Computation in Stylometry II: An Application to the Works of Shakespeare and Marlowe" Vol. 9, No. 1, 1994.

A SHAKESPEARE TIMELINE

Year: Event(s) and Comments:

1564 Birth of William Shakespeare At Stratford-on-

Avon, eldest son of John Shakespeare, April 23rd.

1581 A "Will Shake-shaft" is mentioned as working as an "Antick" or puppeteer in Lancaster.

1582 Marriage of William Shakespeare to Anne Hathaway, license issued November 27th to marry Anne Whateley. License issued November 28th to marry Hathaway.

1583 Susanna, their oldest daughter born, christened May 26th.

1585 Shakespeare twins, Hamet and Judith born; christened Feb. 2.

1586 Shakespeare leaves his home and family around this time (some chroniclers suggest a year earlier) and goes to London.

1587-92 Sir William Davenant, Robert Greene and others describe Shakespeare establishing himself as a player, horse-handler (groome), puppeteer, userer, broker and "Johannes Factotum."

1589 In the above capacities, Shakespeare becomes affiliated with the amalgamated Lord Strange's and Admiral's Men (continuing until 1594).

1592 Robert Greene publishes *A Groats-worth of Wit* warning his fellow playwrights not to do business with the "Upstart Crow" named "Shake-scene." Greene dies of food poisoning a short time later.

1593 Venus and Adonis, registered anonymously in April, is published in June, one week after the death of Marlowe. Shakespeare claims it as the "first heir of his invention" in his dedication to the Earl of Southhampton in September.

1594 Shakespeare described in Willobie his Avisa as having been involved in some way with someone named "H.W.," presumably Henry Wriothsley, the Earl of Southhampton.

1595 Shakespeare living in Bishopsgate, now listed as a partner ("sharer") in the Lord Chamberlain's Men.

1596 Shakespeare's son Hamnet dies.

1597 Richard II published, first Quarto published under Shakespeare's name.

Shakespeare fined in conjunction with his purchase of the New Place in Stratford.

Shakespeare cited for tax evasion in St. Helens parish, London.

1598 Frances Meres, a part-time minister, publishes Palladis Tamia and mentions plays ascribed to Shakespeare on p. 281.

Shakespeare indicted for hoarding grain ("malt") during a famine in Stratford.

1600 Shakespeare sues John Clayton for seven pounds lent in 1592, the year of Greene's invective against Shakespeare the "userer."

1601 Essex Rebellion occurs in London. Participants and authors of the performance of Richard II indicted. Essex executed, Augustine Phillips arrested. Shakespeare ignored by authorities because the Queen knew the playwright to be the "atheist," Marlowe.

1612 Shakespeare gives deposition in Mountjoy lawsuit, regarding a fiscal dispute in a household where he had been a lodger in 1604. He can't remember anything.

1613 Shakespeare leases lands to a neighbor for sheep-grazing, in the "Shakespeare-Replingham Agreement."

1616 Shakespeare writes his will, has a "sound memory" and leaves his "second best bed" to his wife. No mention of plays, poems, books, or writing materials of any kind. Stratford resident John Hall notes in passing that his father-in-law William Shakespeare "died on Thursday."

On Sale Now!

E.C. AYRES'S
TONY LOWELL MYSTERIES
BOOKS 1 – 3

For more information
visit: www.SpeakingVolumes.us

On Sale Now!

**JOHN DEDAKIS'S
LARK CHADWICK MYSTERIES**

**For more information
visit:** www.SpeakingVolumes.us

www.ingramcontent.com/pod-product-compliance
Lightning Source LLC
LaVergne TN
LVHW011223080426
835509LV00005B/283
* 9 7 8 1 6 4 5 4 0 4 1 7 0 *